LEGAL WRITING

IN A NUTSHELL

Third Edition

By

LYNN BAHRYCH, J.D., PH.D.
Attorney at Law

MARJORIE DICK ROMBAUER
Professor Emeritus of Law
School of Law, University of Washington

THOMSON

WEST

Mat # 40133031

COPYRIGHT © 1982 WEST PUBLISHING CO.
COPYRIGHT © 1996 By WEST PUBLISHING CO.
COPYRIGHT © 2003 By West, a Thomson business
            610 Opperman Drive
            P.O. Box 64526
            St. Paul, MN 55164–0526
            1–800–328–9352

ISBN 0–314–14580–X

For Max Thomas Bahrych and Glee C. Bahrych

*

PREFACE

The first edition of this *Nutshell* reflected the combined efforts of Professor of Law Marjorie D. Rombauer, now Emeritus, and Legal Writing Associate Lynn Bahrych Squires, Ph.D., now Lynn Bahrych, attorney at law. Published in 1982, the first edition grew out of their collaborative efforts teaching legal writing and research at the University of Washington School of Law from 1978 until 1982.

Like the prior editions, this third edition is intended to assist law students and experienced lawyers to write more plainly, precisely, efficiently, and effectively. The advent of computer technology and other innovations in communication have changed the context in which lawyers write, but the fundamentals of clear and precise writing remain the same. Therefore, this third edition retains much of the technical content of the first edition concerning the elements of composition. New sections address the twenty-first century lawyer's need to compose and edit easily on a computer screen.

We continue to be indebted to Professor William F. Irmscher of the University of Washington Department of English, the author of two of our sources, *The Holt Guide to English* and *Teaching Expository Writing*. Professor Irmscher read and

PREFACE

commented extensively on the text of the first edition, much of which is retained here. Although a great deal of the work that Professor Rombauer did for the first edition is also retained, she did not participate in the revisions or the new material in this edition. We also wish to thank Professor Kate O'Neill of the University of Washington School of Law and Professor Jeanne Merino, Senior Instructor of Legal Research and Writing at Stanford University School of Law, for their assistance in determining what to include in this edition. A special thanks goes to Jane Ellis of Orcas Island for excellent typing and technical support.

LYNN BAHRYCH, J.D., PH.D.

Seattle, Washington
2003

INTRODUCTION

Lawyers are professional writers. Writing is an essential part of a practicing attorney's daily work. Rather than decreasing the need for writing, the internet and other data transmission innovations have dramatically increased the flow of written communication. The twenty-first century will continue to bring new technologies to the practice of law, but the law will always require the certainty of the written word.

In this century, lawyers must not only write more often, but also more quickly. This new *Nutshell* offers a method of writing clearly, simply, and quickly, with or without a computer. New ethical issues created by the ease of data transmission are addressed in several chapters. Chapters 2 through 6, essentially unchanged from the first edition, provide a condensed handbook for legal writers. These chapters explain the traditional elements of written composition, from organization of a legal document to individual word choices. A glossary of words commonly misused in legal writing is provided in Chapter 5. Diagramming of sentences has been added to the section on grammar in chapter 6 for readers wishing to improve their understanding of the structure of the English language. This new edition includes a simple method of analyzing and improving personal writing style in Chapter 7. The most common forms of legal writing, the research memorandum, client letter, and persuasive brief, are discussed in Chapters 8 and 9.

SUMMARY OF OUTLINE

―――

OUTLINE

XI

Page

Page

*

LEGAL WRITING
IN A NUTSHELL
Third Edition

*

CHAPTER 1

BASIC PRINCIPLES OF LEGAL WRITING

§ 1.1 INTRODUCTION

This chapter provides a brief overview of the basic principles of clear, precise, and effective legal writing. These principles are expanded in Chapters 2 through 9 of this *Nutshell*. The six basic principles introduced below provide the framework for the individual writing analysis in Chapter 7 and apply to all aspects and types of legal writing.

§ 1.2 FIRST PRINCIPLE: THINK, THEN WRITE

Finish your analysis before beginning to write. Identify your audience. Think about how your audience will use what you write.

§ 1.3 SECOND PRINCIPLE: PUT FIRST THINGS FIRST

Make a list of the points you need to make or the purposes of your writing. With the needs of your audience in mind, organize these points or purposes by putting the ones that are most important to your readers first. Usually this means stating your conclusions first.

1

After you have organized your list of points, check to make sure that you do not have the same or similar subjects in different places. Check the list to ensure that related subjects are discussed as closely together as possible, as well as in the order of their importance.

§ 1.4   THIRD PRINCIPLE: ANSWER THE QUESTION, THEN EXPLAIN

Most types of legal writing provide answers to legal questions. Most readers want to know the answers immediately. This includes clients reading opinion letters and judges reading briefs. Answers should be given first, before supporting analysis or discussion.

§ 1.5   FOURTH PRINCIPLE: USE SHORT, SIMPLE SENTENCES

Keep sentences as short and simple as possible. Limit sentences to one unit of thought, that is, one subject-verb unit, whenever you can. All writing begins with a "unit of thought." In English, this normally consists of a subject, or actor, and a verb, or action. Units of thought are basically pairs of nouns and verbs. For example, "sun rises" and "jury deliberates" are units of thought. A unit of thought is the basic building block of communication in the English language.

The first step in writing a simple sentence is to decide who or what will do something or be something. For readers, units of thought are best conveyed with a minimum of added information. A reader more quickly and easily understands the thought expressed by "sun rises" than by "behind the mountain, the winter sun, bringing little heat to the earth, gradually rises." There is, of course, a place for rhetorical flourishes in persuasive writing, as discussed in Chapter 9. For the most part, however, the reader wishes to receive information quickly and concisely, with a minimum of extra words. If your sentence must be complex in structure or must contain several units of thought, try to use repetitive structures, such as parallelism, as discussed in Chapter 4. Parallelism is simply a repetition of the order and types of words.

To save writing and reading time, the legal writer should identify the main subject and main verb (or predicate) in each sentence before writing it. Wherever possible, each sentence should begin with the noun or agent, as discussed in Chapter 4. For more information about the subject and predicate of a sentence and how to identify them, see the section on grammatical diagramming in Chapter 6.

§ 1.6   FIFTH PRINCIPLE: USE SIM-PLE, ORDINARY WORDS AND USE THEM CONSISTENTLY

Select the simplest, shortest words to express your ideas. Common words are best. Legalese should be avoided in favor of ordinary language and common usage. Suggestions for avoiding legalese are offered in Chapter 5. Short words are easy to read and understand and should be chosen whenever possible. To avoid confusion or ambiguity, the same words should always be used to refer to the same things. Unlike other forms of writing, legal writing does not benefit from the use of synonyms or interesting variations of language. Legal writers should repeat nouns rather than using pronouns, even if it seems cumbersome. For the reader, it is easier to comprehend than trying to decide whether a different word implies a slightly different meaning. Use repetitive language even though it may be tedious for you as the writer. Readers of technical material find repetitive language easy to comprehend.

Similarly, use different words to refer to different things. For lawyers, different words indicate different legal concepts. As discussed throughout Chapter 5, careful word choice is an essential ingredient of legal writing.

§ 1.7 SIXTH PRINCIPLE: REPEAT, REPEAT, REPEAT

Repetition is crucial to communication, especially in a complex field such as law. The classical formula for oral argument is to state what you intend to say, say it, then state what you have said. For many types of legal writing, including those discussed in Chapters 8 and 9, this formula should be followed.

Repetition assists the reader, whether it is repetition of the same word to express the same concept, repetition of sentence structure to increase readability, or repetition of content for clarity or emphasis.

CHAPTER 2
LARGE–SCALE ORGANIZATION

§ 2.1 INTRODUCTION

All writing must be organized on several levels. Even a one-sentence statute must have a structure, that is, an order of parts that communicates a thought rather than a jumble of words, phrases, and clauses. The larger the unit of writing, the more levels on which the writing must be organized. Thus, sentences must be arranged within paragraphs. Paragraphs must be arranged in paragraph blocks to present larger units of thought. In extended writings, paragraph blocks and other individual paragraphs must then be arranged within sections and the sections presented in a rational order for the final whole. The organization at each level will reflect relationships between different parts of the whole.

§ 2.2 ORGANIZATION AND ETHICAL ISSUES FOR WRITING ON A COMPUTER

Although the law changes slowly, the technology used for legal writing has changed rapidly. In a relatively short time, law students and practicing lawyers have found themselves spending much of their professional time in front of a computer, whether reading or writing. Consequently, revising and editing of legal writing has become more difficult, especially if documents are sent directly from one computer to another without being printed. Although this *Nutshell* provides a simple and efficient writing method that will work on a computer screen, there is no substitute for organizing, revising, and editing on a printed page.

Keeping the whole of a document in mind while working on a computer is difficult. The process of drafting and revising on a computer screen is limited by the size of the screen. A printed copy should be used to ensure coherence in a document longer than a few paragraphs. Each paragraph should fit like a building block in a well-crafted house. Paragraphs, paragraph blocks, and sections must be viewed as a whole, not simply screen by screen. A useful time to print a document is after the first draft is finished. Each paragraph can then be checked against the outline of the whole. Principles for effective organization of paragraphs are discussed in the following sections of this chapter. Reorganization based on review of a printed draft can easily be done on the computer.

Special care must be taken when copying text from other sources and inserting it into your documents. First, the ethical issue of plagiarism: the ease of copying and inserting and the sheer number of people using data online has made plagiarism both easier to do and harder to prevent. To avoid this unethical practice, legal writers should *always use quotation marks to identify any words that are not their own.* When material is copied, whether from case law or otherwise, the source must be included, either in a footnote or in the text. The exact page or section number must also be identified. For all legal sources, a pinpoint citation is essential. A pinpoint citation is the specific page or section number from which you have taken a statement or other information. Writers who do not provide pinpoint citations are creating unnecessary work for their readers who wish to find the quoted material.

Second, inserted material is foreign matter, like dust in the writer's eye. It was not part of the writer's own vision, nor did it grow from the writer's own chain of thought. Writing is an organic, evolutionary process. Grafting someone else's words onto your own requires a careful use of transitions and a clear view of the whole substance of your writing. Current technology makes it easy to patch sentences, paragraphs, or entire pages in to a memorandum or brief, but this can interrupt the reader's sense of direction and create a confusing mix of tone. Every writer creates a "voice" in the mind of the reader. Introducing new voices requires time, attention to tone, attention to large-scale organization, and conscientious source attribution.

Third, boilerplate should be inserted sparingly and with special care. Both statutes and case law change every day. Yesterday's legally sufficient boilerplate may become tomorrow's malpractice claim. If the boilerplate contains a useful concept or principle, restate it in your own words and cite the source. If the boilerplate contains specific wording that you need, be certain to read it carefully before inserting it. If possible, condense and simplify the wording as a favor to your reader. Again, if you rephrase borrowed material, always cite the source unless it is unquestionably intended to be used without acknowledgement.

Larger units of organization are discussed in the balance of this chapter. Emphasis is on the overall framework of advisory and argumentative writings and the larger units within that framework.

§ 2.3 BASIC PRINCIPLES OF ORGANIZATION

Appropriate organization for a large piece of writing will depend on such special considerations as the form and type of writing, its purpose, the subject matter, and the person to whom it is addressed (the "audience"). Nevertheless, a few basic principles can be followed unless those special considerations suggest different organizing principles. The basic principles are stated in this section. Ways in which the special considerations may affect these basic principles are then discussed in the following sections.

(a) Introduce, Explain, Conclude

Both objective and argumentative legal writing should normally follow the traditional forensic pattern: They should introduce what will be said, say it, and then summarize what was said. This pattern should also be used within sections of an extended writing.

(b) Put Essential Things First

Whatever the form or purpose of a legal writing, it should deal first with the essentials, those matters that are necessary to an understanding of what follows. In the following example, the essential governing principles are stated first to introduce discussion of a problem.

A contract entered into under duress may be avoided by a person who acted under duress. *See generally Restatement of Contracts* §§ 494–495 (1932). Modern authorities agree that a good faith threat of criminal prosecution may be the basis for finding that duress induced a person to enter into a contract. *See generally Restatement of Contracts* § 493 and Comment b (1932); 13 *Williston on Contracts* §§ 1611–15 (3d ed. W. Jaeger 1970). The primary questions presented in our client's case stem from the Washington court's inconsistency in considering whether such a threat may constitute duress as a matter of law.

Factual considerations as well as legal principles may be essentials when, for example, the resolution of a problem will ultimately turn on the resolution of a factual question or the result of future investigations.

The crucial question in this case is whether our client promised to arrange for transfer of the fire insurance policy covering the warehouse sold to the plaintiffs. If a promise was made, two theories may support a recovery for the plaintiff. The testimony of the lender's attorney, the only disinterested witness, will probably be more favorable to the plaintiff than to our client on this question. The following discussion is therefore based on an assumption that a judge or jury would find that a promise had been made.

Putting essential matters first is important to maintain reader interest as well as to aid reader understanding. The legal writer must get to the essentials quickly or risk losing the reader's attention. This is true whether that reader is a judge, a law clerk, a client, or another lawyer.

(c) Keep Related Matters Together

Order of presentation can suggest relationships indirectly, even though the relationships are not expressly stated. It can also reinforce explicit statements about relationships. Therefore, a large part of deciding on appropriate organization is identifying the relationships to be communicated. After relationships are identified, an organization that keeps related matters together should be planned.

(d) Use Headings and Transitions

Headings and subheadings are necessary aids to keep the reader informed of subject matter changes. Topic headings should be used for major divisions. Subheadings may be used to identify the topic of a paragraph or block of paragraphs. In addition to headings, explicit transitions should be included to guide the reader from point to point and from question to question. These may be transitional words, sentences or paragraphs. See the section on transitions in Chapter 3.

§ 2.4   ORGANIZATION OF ADVISORY AND ARGUMENTATIVE WRITING

Both advisory and argumentative writing consist of several basic ingredients: facts, questions, authorities, rules, rationales, applications, and conclusions. These ingredients shape the organization of most forms of legal writing. For example, compare the following outlines for standard law office memorandum form and for United States Supreme Court brief form. (Some preliminary sections are omitted as not relevant to the immediate discussion.)

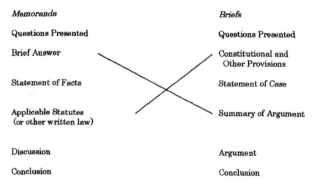

Memoranda	*Briefs*
Questions Presented	Questions Presented
Brief Answer	Constitutional and Other Provisions
Statement of Facts	Statement of Case
Applicable Statutes (or other written law)	Summary of Argument
Discussion	Argument
Conclusion	Conclusion

Note that the order is the same for the key sections: questions, facts, discussion/argument, and conclusion.

§ 2.5 ORGANIZATION OF DIS-CUSSION OR ARGUMENT SECTIONS

(a) Introduction

The heart of advisory writing is the Discussion section, and the heart of argumentative writing is the Argument section. In these sections, the questions presented will be restated and explained; relevant authorities will be cited and discussed; policies, rules, and rationales will be examined and applied to the significant facts; and specific conclusions will be stated.

If a problem or case presents more than one question, the order in which the Questions Presented and subquestions are stated will provide the basic framework. Therefore, the first decision about organization is the appropriate order of discussion for the questions. The following principles and examples provide some guidelines for that decision. The examples are taken from law office memoranda. If the goal is to persuade, as in an appellate brief, these organizational patterns may be altered for rhetorical effect. (See Chapter 9.)

(b) Interdependent or Other Logical Order

(1) Interdependent Questions

Sometimes the existence of a question or the answer to a question will depend on the answer to another question. Discussion of the prior question first will usually make the interrelationship easier for the reader to understand and will avoid awkward cross-referencing.

> "Our client sold a pet store that was later destroyed by fire. The buyer, Tomoe Minamoto, alleges that at the time the sale was closed, our client promised to arrange for transfer of her fire insurance policy for the benefit of the buyer."

Question: May the client be liable to the buyer for the full loss for failing to perform the alleged promise?

1. Did our client promise Ms. Minamoto to arrange for transfer of the insurance policy? (fact question)

2. Assuming that our client did promise, was the promise sufficiently definite to be enforceable?

3. Assuming that a sufficiently definite promise was made, would the parole evidence rule make evidence of the oral promise inadmissible, or would the exception for subsequent or separate agreements apply?

4. If evidence of the oral promise is admissible, would the promise be enforceable without Ms. Minamoto having given or promised consideration for it?

   a. Would the promise be enforceable under the promissory estoppel doctrine?

   b. Would a promissory duty be enforced under the *Hudson* gratuitous agency rule?

(2) Chronological Order

If questions are related to a chronology of events, discussion in the order in which events occurred will often facilitate understanding.

EXAMPLE 1:

A Did our client, Roger, tortiously induce Tom to breach a contract for exchange of his boat for Savvy's boat?

    1. Did a valid contract exist between Savvy and Tom at the time Roger first discussed trading his boat for Tom's boat on September 15th, or had the Savvy–Tom contract already been breached by repudiation on September 14th?

    2. Assuming that a valid contract did exist on September 15th, did Roger's conduct in offering to exchange his boat on similar terms, making disparaging remarks about Savvy's boat, and contracting with Tom for exchange of their boats constitute the kind of interference that may be the basis for a tort action?

    3. Was Roger's conduct privileged because he was a "competitor"?

B. Did Roger's conduct in taking Tom's boat from Savvy's dock on September 18th induce or cause termination of a valid business expectancy?

EXAMPLE 2:

A. Must evidence of remarriage of a plaintiff in a wrongful death action be excluded as irrelevant?

B. Even though such evidence would otherwise be excluded, can questions about plaintiff's new spouse be asked during *voir dire* to ascertain prospective jurors' possible acquaintance with the new spouse?

(3) Authority Value Order

Ordinarily, questions governed by different forms of law should be discussed in the order of the authority value of the form: constitutional questions should be discussed first, then statutory questions, and then common law questions, because constitutional provisions would ordinarily override statutory provisions, and statutory provisions would ordinarily override prior common law. This order may be altered, however, by the source of a question. For example, a possible interpretation of a statute may create a constitutional question, requiring that the statutory interpretation question be discussed first. The same change in order may be suggested by a court's preference for avoiding constitutional questions if a possible interpretation of a statute might make decision of the constitutional question unnecessary. Also, the need to determine the meaning of a common law concept incorporated in a statute may require that common law precedents defining the concept be discussed first.

Interwoven with the order suggested by forms of law may be the order suggested by levels of governmental source of authority. Thus, federal questions and authorities would ordinarily be discussed first, then state questions and authorities, and then authorities from lower governmental units.

Intermixed with both the form and source of authority may be another hierarchy of authority, that is, mandatory and persuasive sources (for common law questions, for example) and secondary sources. If, however, mandatory authorities are not directly in point and persuasive or secondary authorities are, then this order, too, may be altered.

(4) Conceptual or Rule Element Order

Statutory and other rules may incorporate several elements that must be established before the statute or rule can be said to govern resolution of a particular problem. If questions are presented for more than one element, discussion in the order the elements appear in the statute or rule may be the appropriate order.

(c) Order of Importance

Order of importance will be influenced by the particular writing task. In a brief, the strongest argument will usually be the most important. In a memorandum prepared to help an attorney decide whether to institute litigation, the weakest link may be the most important. Ultimately, you will find that decisions about the relative importance of ideas or arguments must be based on thorough understanding of the substance of particular problems.

No general writing principles can guide you in making such decisions.

(d) Order of Request

If you have been asked to discuss particular questions, and if those questions have no natural order or variation in importance, then follow the order suggested in the request. Such requests may come from another attorney (as for law office memoranda) or from a judge (as for a memorandum on evidentiary questions that have arisen during a trial). If the request comes from a judge, strategies for persuasion may suggest a different order. (See Chapter 9.)

§ 2.5 PRINCIPLES OF ORGANIZATION FOR INDIVIDUAL QUESTIONS

(a) Use Basic Analytical Organization Absent Special Considerations

For each Question Presented, there is a predetermined analytical content for discussion or argument: The question will be stated and explained; authorities will be cited and discussed; rules, rationales, and policies will be explained and applied to the significant facts; and specific conclusions will be expressed. This predetermined content also suggests an organization for discussion of each question.

The suggested organization is illustrated in the following discussion of a simple legal question. For more difficult questions, each part may require its own paragraph or block of paragraphs.

Conclusion

Our client did not tortiously induce breach of the Savvy–Tom contract.

Specific Question and answer

The basic question is whether a contract that has been consistently repudiated by the maker (as by Tom in this case) is the kind of contractual relationship protected by the tortious interference rule. It is not. See

Authorities

Restatement (Second) of Torts § 766, Comment f (1979); *United States v. Newbury Mfg. Co.*, 36 F.Supp. 602 (D.Mass.1941).

In *Newbury*, the United States had entered into a contract with Defendant Newbury and had delivered goods that Newbury had agreed to dispose of by export to foreign countries only. The United States alleged a breach by Newbury in contracting

Rationale

to sell the goods to Defendant Belmont *and others* in the United States. It also alleged tortious interference by Belmont in inducing breach. In granting Belmont's motion to dismiss for failure to state a claim, the court held that Belmont could not be held liable for tortious interference, stating in part that "The rule [respecting recovery for tortious interference] presupposes that the party defaulting was ready, able, and willing to perform and would have done so if it had not been prevented or persuaded by the malicious and unwarranted interfer-

ence of a third party." 36 F.Supp. at
605.

*Application
To facts*

*Restatement
of
Conclusion*

In our client's case, Tom had failed
and refused to perform his contract
with Savvy continuously for at least
thirteen days before our client allegedly interfered. Therefore, Savvy did
not have the kind of contractual relationship contemplated by the rule
against interference, and our client
could not have tortiously induced
breach of the Savvy–Tom contract.

Although the suggested analytical organization is
often sufficient, special considerations may suggest
variation. For example, if authorities are weak and
policy considerations are strong, policy should be
discussed before authorities under the principle
that the more important matter should appear first.
Then, too, not all questions require discussion of
each part included in the example. Some questions
may require discussion of other types of content, for
example, fact questions that must be discussed before a rule is applied to the significant facts.

(b) Begin with Statement of Your Answer Absent Special Considerations

One feature of the organization suggested in the
preceding subsection should usually not be varied:
Statement of a specific answer to a Question Presented should ordinarily not be deferred beyond the
beginning point. Two reasons dictate this highlight-
ing of conclusions. First, advisory writing is intend-

ed to inform as the basis for advice, and argumentative writing is intended to lead another's thinking as the basis for persuasion. Knowing where a discussion or argument is leading is essential if a reader is to be informed or persuaded. Second, knowing where a discussion or argument is leading is essential if a reader is to understand on first reading. A reader's understanding on first reading is a significant objective for this kind of writing because the reader will almost always want to grasp the material in minimum reading time. In some circumstances, the reader may be required to understand on the basis of scanning rather than careful reading. You should not ordinarily expect your reader to return to a preliminary Brief Answer or Summary of Argument in order to have your conclusions in mind. Neither should your reader have to look ahead to the formal, summarizing Conclusion to determine where you are leading.

Special circumstances may require that statement of an answer be deferred. For example, if you are not sure that your reader understands the subject area about which you are writing, you should provide a background introduction. Similarly, you may need to explain why a question is presented if that is not evident.

§ 2.6   IS AN OUTLINE NECESSARY?

The purpose and form of advisory and argumentative writing will provide a general framework. Must you identify a more detailed structure before you begin writing?

Many writing experts emphatically recommend that writers prepare a formal, detailed outline before beginning to write. However, experienced legal writers may not need a formal outline. Often a written outline is unnecessary because the writer has a sufficient outline in mind. Perhaps the writer understands the subject very well. Perhaps the subject is simple or the subject matter has an inherent structure. Perhaps the writer's notes (research notes, for example) are well structured already. In any event, the writer *is* following a predetermined outline of some sort.

Alternatively, a writer may begin writing with the expectation of developing appropriate structure in the writing process. This approach, too, may ultimately produce a good product. Trying to express one's thoughts may lead to new thoughts. New viewpoints, new syntheses, or new relationships may be recognized. A continuing interaction between the process of writing and the writing itself may lead to recognition of a structure that was not recognized at the beginning. Once an appropriate structure is recognized, the process should be reversed. An outline of the draft, reorganized and filled out with additional details, can then be the starting point for a less tentative draft.

Note, however, that writing in search of structure can be a time-consuming process—and may be an unproductive process. The answer to the question of whether to outline, therefore, is, "Yes, you should try to write an outline if you do not have a clear mental outline of a well understood, simple, or

inherently structured subject." Attempting to outline can also lead to recognition of structure. More
importantly, attempting to write an outline can lead
to a clearer view of what you want to say.

Therefore, unless you have a mental outline, plan
to begin advisory or argumentative writing by outlining at least a general framework. Do not feel
committed to forcing everything into a highly structured outline (that is, in complete sentences, neatly
ordered under an appropriate combination of Ro-
man numerals, capital letters, and so on). Outlining
is an efficient prewriting exercise as long as your
approach remains flexible. The need for details
grows, however, as the complexity of the subject
increases. The greater the prospective writer's uncertainty about the subject, the greater the need to
push the search for structure.

Use of a computer or any type of voice-activated
machine makes outlining more important. Preparing an outline of main points and key phrases
before drafting on a screen or dictating will save
editorial and revision time later.

§ 2.7 ILLUSTRATIVE GENERAL
OUTLINE

The following general outline of a memorandum
discussion is provided to demonstrate some of the
organization principles discussed in this chapter.
The order of discussion for each question might be
altered by one or more other organizational considerations. For example, if the answer to the statuto-

ry question will determine whether there is a constitutional question, the statutory question might be discussed first. An outline for an argument addressed to the same questions might be varied for reasons of persuasion as discussed in Chapter 9.

Background explanation of subject area of problem

Statement of ultimate conclusion

First question (assume a constitutional question)

  Statement of conclusion

  Discussion of authority

    Language of constitution

    Construing court opinions (discussion of holdings, dicta, underlying rules, rationales, and policies)

      Supreme Court, circuit court of appeal

      State appellate courts, federal district courts

  Secondary authorities

  Supporting or countervailing policy considerations

  Applications to facts

  Restatement of conclusion

Second question (assume a statutory question)

  Explanation of statutory language that creates the question

  Statement of conclusion

  Discussion of authority

    Legislative history

    Construing court opinions

  Application to facts

  Restatement of conclusion

Third question (assume a common law question)

Statement of conclusion

Explain why question is presented

Discussion of authorities

Mandatory precedents (discussion of holdings, dicta, underlying rules, and rationales of the courts of the jurisdiction whose law controls)

Policy considerations

Persuasive authorities (discussion of holdings, dicta and so on from courts of other jurisdictions)

Secondary authorities

Conclusion (summarizing and relating the answers to the individual questions and restating the ultimate conclusion)

CHAPTER 3

SMALL–SCALE ORGANIZATION: PARAGRAPHS, PARAGRAPH BLOCKS, AND TRANSITIONS

§ 3.1 INTRODUCTION

Small-scale organization is the ordering of paragraphs or paragraph blocks, joined by transitions. A paragraph block is several paragraphs that develop a single, major topic. In this chapter, the basic principles of paragraph organization will be summarized, followed by a discussion of paragraph blocks. The chapter concludes with a review of transitional devices.

§ 3.2 BASIC PRINCIPLES OF PARAGRAPH ORGANIZATION

(a) Introduction

Just as overall organization of a discussion or argument communicates meaning, so does paragraph structure. Readers expect, for example, that a paragraph will have a governing theme (a "topic") and that the first sentence in the paragraph will state the topic. This expectation parallels the standard paragraph pattern: The topic sentence, usually the first, introduces the paragraph theme; the remaining sentences elaborate on it. In longer paragraphs, the final sentence may recapitulate the theme or offer a conclusion.

While we as readers look for the standard paragraph pattern, as writers we do not always provide it. Most writers paragraph intuitively, basing their decisions to break on a sense of closure. Most of the time, a good writer's intuition will result in clear and meaningful paragraph division. Good writers will have more control and more consistent success, however, if they understand the principles that they intuitively observe.

We paragraph for several reasons: (i) for logical divisions, for example, separation of issues or case analyses, (ii) for rhetorical purposes, and (ii) for visual effect. These often overlap. In legal writing, paragraphing normally should reflect logical divisions. Much of legal writing consists of the development of an argument or of analysis of an issue through logical steps. Those steps make up individual paragraphs while the argument as a whole makes up a block of paragraphs.

Like punctuation in general, paragraphing is a matter of desired effect as well as of interpretation. A series of long paragraphs, for example, invites a short one for contrast and emphasis. A series of short paragraphs invites a single expansive one.

(b) Use Meaningful Paragraph Blocks

Paragraph blocks in legal writing are usually more important structural divisions than individual paragraphs. Traditional discussions of paragraphing are therefore inadequate for the legal writer who must organize groups of paragraphs into sections and subsections of memoranda and briefs. The commonplace Issue–Rule–Application–Conclusion ("IRAC") paragraph pattern described below, for example, typically requires a block of two or more paragraphs and only rarely can be managed in a single paragraph. Similarly, the comparison and contrast paragraph pattern used to analyze facts in a series of cases generally requires several paragraphs.

Paragraph blocks are groups of paragraphs that together present a major point. They may consist of two or of a dozen or more paragraphs. They may fall under a single subheading, or several blocks may fall under the same subheading. A heading identifying the theme of the block is customary and helpful.

Combining groups of paragraphs is particularly difficult on a computer screen or while dictating. Most writers need to work from a printed page in order to manage paragraphs effectively.

A paragraph block often begins with a paragraph introducing the theme or topic of the block. The following paragraphs then develop that theme. The paragraph block is thus frequently an expansion of the standard pattern: the standard topic sentence expanded into a paragraph, the supporting sentences into separate paragraphs, and the concluding sentence expanded into a concluding paragraph.

This expansion allows for a more detailed discussion of substance without interminable paragraphs.

The legal writer may not need to plan such paragraph blocks in advance. A block of related paragraphs will develop during the writing process. After a draft is completed, however, the writer should check to see if the paragraph pattern will be intelligible to the reader. That is, the writer should print the draft in order to identify (perhaps by outlining roughly) the paragraph blocks, check for a governing major theme, and check transitions between component paragraphs.

Although legal writers need not design paragraph blocks in advance or attempt to construct them while writing, they should work consciously to link inner parts, that is, to tie paragraphs together. Identifying transitional elements is part of the analytical task of the legal writer; such elements are essential for a reader's comprehension.

(c) Avoid Excesses in Paragraph Length

Within a paragraph block, a paragraph is a mark of punctuation. Like the period, the last sentence of a paragraph marks closure of a theme. The theme of a paragraph must be one that can be stated, developed, and closed within a unit of writing long enough to hold interest but short enough to be read and understood as a unit. If a reader must reread a paragraph to grasp the theme, then the paragraph is too long. If a paragraph or series of paragraphs presents a chopped-up theme, then the paragraphs are too short. No mechanical rule can provide a guide for the writer to know when a paragraph is "too long" or "too short." If a paragraph is longer than half a standard 250–word page, consider dividing it. Remember that readers appreciate the mental break that a new paragraph provides.

(d) Use One– or Two–Sentence Paragraphs Sparingly

Just as the very short sentence lends emphasis to a point, so a single-sentence paragraph lends emphasis to its content. Such paragraphs should be used sparingly for special effect. They may highlight a major transition, emphasize an important conclusion, or summarize a block of paragraphs.

(e) Use the First and Last Sentences as Positions of Emphasis

The most important ideas should appear in the first and last sentences of a paragraph. These sentences will usually be the more general statements, with more detailed ones in the middle of the paragraph.

(f) Avoid Placing Full Citations in the Positions of Emphasis

Because the first and last sentences are positions of greatest emphasis within a paragraph, to clutter them with legal citations is to distract form the point. Note how the citation delays attention to the substance of the following sentences.

In *Allen v. Ennis,* 253 App.Div. 769, 300 N.Y.S.2d 1323 (3d Dept. 1937), a commission employee of the defendant automobile dealer negligently caused the death of the passenger while demonstrating a car. He was convicted of negligent homicide despite his lack of actual knowledge of the car defect that contributed to the fatal accident. His status as an employee did not alter his responsibility to be aware of the limitations of the vehicle that he was driving.

When an authority is the theme of a paragraph, as in the *Allen v. Ennis* paragraph, the writer should attempt to characterize the authority by subject matter, source, or other significant detail. Then the citation may be stated as a separate sentence or as the last part of the topic sentence.

Revision of the above example: In another negligent homicide prosecution [or, In a New York case, or, In an early case] a commission employee of the defendant automobile dealer had negligently caused the death of the passenger while demonstrating a car. *Allen v. Ennis,* 253 App.Div. 769, 300 N.Y.S.2d 1323 (3d Dept. 1937). [Note the treatment of this separate citation as a sentence by use of a period at the end.]

§ 3.3   STANDARD PARAGRAPH AND PARAGRAPH BLOCK PATTERNS

(a) TEC Pattern: Topic Sentence, Elaboration, Conclusion

In the standard paragraph, the first sentence introduces or signals the topic. If you cannot summarize the topic or subject of a paragraph in a single sentence, then you are including too much in the paragraph. The topic sentence is customarily followed by supporting discussion, which may be an illustration, example, analysis, or explanation. A conclusion may or may not end the paragraph.

Topic sentences stating a legal proposition:

1. "Willful" means more than merely involuntary action.

2. A prior restraint regulation must contain precise criteria, spelling out what is forbidden.

Topic sentences phrased as direct or indirect questions:

1. Did the court have jurisdiction under the general statute?

2. The question is whether the three-year or the six-year limitation should be applied.

Topic sentences phrased as conclusions:

1. Our client will have no right to reject future deliveries if it accepts the present consignment.

2. Our client's conduct will probably not be found to have been reasonable.

T E *Example of TEC paragraph:* The decisional scheme of the Citing Act should not be subject to review despite the provisions of that Act for judicial review. The scheme is similar to that held by the Supreme Court to be non-reviewable in *Chicago & Southern Air Lines, Inc. v. Waterman S. S. Corp.*, 333 U.S. 103 (1948). In that case the Court considered a clause in the Civil Aeronautics Act that provided, as does the Citing Act, that certain orders of the Civil Aeronautics Board (CAB) were subject to the approval of the President. The Supreme Court held that because this clause created an implied exception to the same Act that provided for judicial review of the CAB's orders, the CAB's orders were not reviewable. The Court reasoned that the President's decision, necessary to the effectiveness of the CAB's order, was political, not judicial, and hence not reviewable. 333 U.S. at 111. Since the

C   decisional scheme in the Citing Act is based on a similar clause, making approval of citing a political rather than a judicial decision, this scheme should not be subject to review.

(b) ET Pattern: Elaboration, Topic

This variation of the standard pattern provides an inductive structure: first the support or elaboration is given, then the topic. The topic statement at the end functions like a conclusion. Since this pattern leaves the reader guessing what the point will be, it should be used advisedly. One possible use is for introductory or concluding paragraphs. In an introductory paragraph, the inductive pattern allows the writer to lead the reader into a subject by using particulars that build to a generalization. This may be advantageous if the reader might otherwise find it difficult to believe the generalization or if the reader is likely to resist the generalization initially. In a concluding paragraph, the inductive pattern presents no mystery since, presumably, the reader has already comprehended the discussion or analysis that is being summarized. A summary ET paragraph may also serve as a rhetorical device to emphasize an important conclusion. In general, however, the ET or inductive pattern of paragraph development frustrates the reader.

(c) IRAC Pattern: Issue, Rule, Application of Rule to Facts, Conclusion

The basic structure for an analytical paragraph or paragraph block includes (i) the issue, (ii) the governing rules of law, (iii) relevant facts, (iv) application of law to facts, and (v) conclusion or summary of statement.

For an effective IRAC paragraph, the issue must be stated, usually in the topic sentence. The issue statement should precede statement of the rule or the governing law. An application of the rule to the facts should follow the rule or the governing law. The content of each paragraph or paragraph block should be summarized at the end.

I   *Example of IRAC:* The issue is whether police seizure of a presumably stolen television set can be justified under the plain view doctrine. The court has held
R   that such seizure can be justified if an officer has knowledge that the goods are stolen. In *State v. Keefe,* the court found that the seizure of a typewriter that came into plain view during the proper search of Keefe's residence was unjustified. Although the officers suspected that the defendant was part of a forgery ring that made use of a typewriter, they did not have immediate knowledge that the typewriter was evidence of the crime. The court found that the typewriter was merely an item of "possible evidentiary value" and, as such, could not be the subject of
A   further search or seizure. Similarly, the television set in our case is, at best, of only "possible" evidentiary value. Since the officers did not know that the set had been stolen, the warrantless seizure of the set
C   cannot be justified by relying on the plain view doctrine.

(d) PS Pattern: Problem, Solution

If a paragraph begins with the statement of a problem, the reader expects some indication of its solution before the paragraph closes.

P *Example of PS*: The District needed to establish the starting and ending times of the 1976–77 student day by August 1, 1976. Without determining the duration of the student day, the District was unable to arrange course offerings and schedules, arrange and test bus routes, engage sufficient busses, notify bus drivers of route bidding, inform the public of bus routes and times, coordinate special education programs with surrounding school districts, hire and assign personnel, and so forth. The striking teachers' union was unwilling to recommence negotiations or to meet with the Board. Consequently, on July 10 the Board
S approved the 1976–77 student day as developed and recommended by the administration. The starting and ending times, based on many operational considerations, are shown below.

(e) Comparison and Contrast Patterns

Legal analysis frequently requires comparisons and contrasts, that is, explanations of similarities and differences between cases, fact patterns, laws, or theories. Comparisons may be as broad as in Model One below or as narrow as in Model Three. The structure chosen should reflect the degree of detail or the fineness of analysis required by the subject matter.

Model One provides a general, not a detailed, comparison. The limitation of this model is that the reader will not remember all the points made in paragraph A while reading paragraph B.

Model One: ¶ *One (Theory A) followed by*

¶ *Two (Theory B)*

¶ *One, Theory A*

Even though the Council was not required to consider alternative sites for the power plant, it nevertheless did so. Such consideration was more than sufficient to meet any reasonable standard. The evidence on alternative sites was extensive. For example, the evidence included a comprehensive point-by-point evaluation of the Valley site in comparison with the two potential sites considered to be the next best. After weighing this evidence, the Council found that none of the alternatives was "preferable" to the Valley site. Two standards are implicit in the Council's findings: (1) that a site is satisfactory and should be approved unless it appears that another site is clearly preferable and (2) that the Council, as a licensing agency, should approve or reject a proposed site rather than select one for the applicant.

¶ *Two, Theory B*

Petitioners, on the other hand, would have the Council determine which site is the "best" site from among what they refer to as the "available alternative sites." They would require the Council, in each certification proceeding, to recommend rejection of the application unless it can be established that the proposed site is the best available site in the state. They would force applicants and their ratepayers to incur substantial additional costs in selecting, studying, documenting, and evaluating alternative sites. They would apply this standard to the Council's licensing action, even though the agency is empowered only to approve or reject the site proposed by the applicant. Petitioners would have the Council itself choose a site for the applicant.

Model Two requires a strong internal transition, as well as a tighter comparison of A and B. The transition is, "The Petitioners were now, however, satisfied with this finding."

Model Two: ¶ *One, Theory A, then Theory B*

Even though the Council was not required to consider alternative sites for the power plant, it nevertheless did so. Its consideration was more than sufficient to meet any reasonable standard. The evidence on alternative sites was extensive. For example, it included a comprehensive point-by-point evaluation of the Valley site in comparison with the two potential sites considered to be the next best. After weighing this evidence, the Council found that none of the alternatives was preferable to the Valley site. The Petitioners were not, however, satisfied with this finding. Petitioners would have the Council determine which cite is the best site from among those they refer to as the "available alternative sites." They would require the Council, in each certification proceeding, to recommend rejection of the application unless it can be established that the proposed site is the best available site in the state. This would force applicants and their ratepayers to incur substantial additional costs in selecting, studying, documenting, and evaluating alternative sites. It would require a degree of precision in evaluation and comparison of sites that is presently unattainable. Thus, the Council properly rejected the "best" site standard.

In Model Three, A and B are compared on three levels or in terms of three subtopics. This model requires five transitions (as opposed to one) between A and B. It is accordingly more difficult to write but allows for more detailed comparison and contrast.

Model Three: ¶ Block, AB, AB, AB, A

A   Even through the Council was not required to consider alternative sites, it nevertheless did so. The extensive evidence collected on alternative sites included a comprehensive point-by-point evaluation of the Valley site in comparison with the two potential sites considered to be the next best. After weighing
B   this evidence, the Council found that none of the alternatives was "preferable" to the Valley site. Petitioners, on the other hand, would have the Council determine which site is the "best" from among what they refer to as the "available alternative sites."

A   This "best site" standard would force applicants
     and their ratepayers to incur substantial additional
B   costs in selecting, studying, documenting, and evalu-
     ating alternative sites. Although, as Petitioners
     claim, the standard requires a greater degree of preci-
     sion in evaluating and comparing sites than the
     Council's own standard, that degree of precision is
     presently unattainable.

A   Whether or not the "best" site standard is feasible,
     the Council is not empowered to employ it. The
     Council, as a licensing agency, may approve or reject
     a proposed site, but not select one for the applicant.
B   Petitioners argue that the Council is responsible for
     selecting, or compelling the selection, of the best
     available site in the state. However, the Council is
     empowered only to approve a satisfactory site, unless
     it appears that another site is clearly preferable.

A   Because the Council has found no preferable alter-
     native, there is no basis in either law or reason for
     the application of petitioners' "best" site standard.
     Therefore, the Council's rejection of this standard is
     proper.

(f) Definition Pattern

This paragraph pattern consists of a detailed definition of a legal concept or area of law. It functions
like the Rule section of an IRAC paragraph. It is
more effective if preceded by a statement of the
issue in an earlier paragraph and if followed by an
application of the definition in a subsequent paragraph.

   Example of Definition Paragraph: An arrest must be
based on probable cause to be lawful. Section
12A.01.140 of the Seattle Criminal Code specifies that
"a peace officer may arrest a person without a warrant

if the officer has *probable cause* to believe that such a person has committed a crime.'' [emphasis supplied] Therefore, a warrantless arrest must be carefully scrutinized to ensure that probable cause exists. *United States v. Ventresca,* 380 U.S. 102, 85 S.Ct. 741, 13 L.Ed.2d 684 (1965). The test for probable cause is whether there is enough information to warrant a man of reasonable caution to believe that a crime has been committed and that the person arrested has committed it. *Carroll v. United States,* 267 U.S. 132, 162, 45 S.Ct. 280, 69 L.Ed. 543 (1925). There is thus a two-part, conjunctive requirement. The officer must have a reasonably certain belief: (1) that a crime has been committed and (2) that the person to be arrested has committed it. [Next paragraph turns to application of this definition.]

§ 3.4 TRANSITIONS

(a) Introduction

A good transition refers to what has preceded and announces what is to follow.

Without transitions, a piece of legal writing is like a mosaic without glue: nothing, no matter how elegantly designed, holds together. With good transitions, even a poorly organized discussion can be understood. For substantive coherence, every sentence should be linked to its surrounding sentences. Every paragraph should be linked to the preceding paragraph, either by theme or by explicit transitional words, unless the writer has moved from one unrelated issue to another. Even then a transition may be needed to signal the lack of relationship if headings are not used.

Transitions between issues, subissues, and paragraph blocks must be carefully constructed. These may be (i) paragraphs in themselves, that is, transitional paragraphs, (ii) the first sentence in a subsequent paragraph, (iii) the last sentence in a preceding paragraph, or (iv) a substantive link between paragraphs.

(b) Transitional Paragraphs

Transitional or "roadmap" paragraphs may be used to link discussion of two issues. Issue discussions are normally separated in memoranda and briefs by major headings that provide a sharp visual break. A transitional paragraph appears at the start of discussion of the second issue or, less commonly, at the end of discussion of the first. The transitional paragraph will be effective at the end of the first issue only if the conclusion for that issue forecasts the discussion of the second issue or leads logically into it. Normally, the first paragraph of the second issue (in which the relationship between the two issues is explained) serves as the transitional paragraph.

If two questions bear no relationship to one another, then the writer should simply regard the first paragraph of the second issue as a fresh start and make no reference to the first issue. The headings and format of the memorandum of brief should provide sufficient visual division.

A transitional paragraph may be used to summarize the content of a paragraph block and to introduce the next paragraph block. Such a paragraph calls attention to an important change of topic, to a shift in the logical sequence of ideas, to a conclusion, or perhaps to a single, telling point. When writing a paragraph meant to link two paragraph blocks, ask yourself: Why go on to the next topic? What is the next logical step?

The most effective transitional paragraphs are those in which the substantive link is clear without the aid of well-worn transitional words and phrases, such as "The next point is" or "Another important theory is."

(c) Transitional Sentences

Two successive paragraphs are most commonly linked by a transitional sentence. The writer must construct paragraphs so that either the first leads into the second or the second refers back to the first. This usually is done in a transitional sentence. An excellent transitional device from the reader's point of view is a sentence summarizing the preceding paragraph. For example, this summary sentence might link two paragraphs: "Although the *Restatement* position dominates the law, one United States Supreme Court case should be considered in the context of employee exculpation." Here again, the least effective transitional sentence is the one beginning with mechanical place-fillers, such as "The next case to be considered is" or "In addition, the court must consider." The best writing achieves fluid transition without using obvious transition words. The best transitions are those that are not conspicuous but rather that are intrinsic to the logic and style of a particular piece of legal writing.

Simple enumeration, as in "First," "Second," "Third," or (1), (2), and (3), does more than place-filling; it provides important information to the reader. This device, often referred to as structured enumeration, is a means of identifying elements or subordinate detail and of showing how the elements relate to significant points. For example, after stating a rule of law, set out the reasons for its value: "This rule is sound for the following reasons." Either number the reasons or introduce each with a "first," "second," or "third." This makes the discussion of the memorandum with others easier as well as making it easier to read.

Parallelism is another simple but useful transitional device. Two sentences containing the same parts of speech arranged in the same order are said to be parallel, for example: "A good defense is based on more than law. A good defense is based on sound principle." Several sentences with a common subject, with or without parallel predicates, will provide smooth reading as well as reflect substantive links between ideas.

(d) Substantive Transitions Between Sentences

A substantive link serves as an excellent transition between sentences.

1. *These holdings,* then, have to be carefully compared.

2. Given *this historical precedent,* the court will undoubtedly affirm the judgment.

3. If *so interpreted,* the new Act will aid our client.

4. From *this analysis,* we may predict a similar outcome in our case.

A summary phrase referring to a subject just discussed provides transition.

1. Plaintiff's position, *that the report should be admitted as evidence,* is consistent with that of the government.

2. Police officers have a proper alternative for investigating facts when, *as in this case, they suspect foul play but have no probable cause to arrest.*

3. This holding, *that federal common law should control the ownership question,* was recently overruled.

4. Just as *the actions were dissimilar in the two cases,* so also were the remedies sought.

Repetition or echo of key words or phrases serves as an effective substantive transition between sentences. Most legal terms of art function as transitions each time they are repeated. Words or phrases such as "life estate" bring to mind a complex concept that need not be restated in full each time the term is used.

The juxtaposition of two case discussions presents a common transition problem. Rather than using the citation of the second case as a crutch to move you from case to case, use substantive information. Identify (i) the similarities or differences between the cases, (ii) their chronological or jurisdictional relationships, (iii) the relative importance of the cases, or (iv) some other substantive link.

1. The Washington Supreme Court gives needed direction to our analysis of the facts in *Bradley* [case discussed in preceding paragraph] in its prior holding in *Arthur v. Court*, 74 Wash.2d 715, 495 P.2d 666 (1979).

2. The Court in *Sisler* further expands the *Borst* decision by ruling that a child may sue the estate of a deceased parent.

3. The Supreme Court expanded and clarified its definition of "interrogation" in *Brewer v. Williams*, 430 U.S. 387 (1977).

(e) Transitional Words

Transitional words must be used precisely. The common transitional words "yet" and "however" are often misused; they signal a change of direction, comparable to "on the other hand." Transitional words that have several possible meanings, such as the general utility word "as," are difficult to use precisely and thus should be avoided. Transitional words with a single narrow meaning, such as "conversely," are extremely useful to the legal writer but must be used appropriately, as in the following example:

> If an employment contract does not provide for a definite period of employment, the employer may discharge the employee at any time, with or without cause. *Conversely*, an employment contract for a definite period of time is not terminable at will.

In the above example, the transitional word "conversely" emphasizes the substance of the sentence it introduces. This substantive dimension is the key to effective transition. The best transitions are logical and substantive, not mechanical place-fillers like "and" or "in addition." They express the logical connection between what went before and what comes after.

(f) Transitions to Avoid: Nonsubstantive Place-fillers

Do not use imprecise, general transitional words or case citations to fill the place of a substantive transition. Citations are attractive because they save the writer the trouble of crafting a transition and often of determining the logical connection between two sentences or paragraphs. An abbreviated case name, for example "In *Williams,*" is often a false transition; it seems to move the reader from idea to idea, but it may merely change the subject.

Examples of Imprecise or Ambiguous Transitions:

1. Plaintiff is factually and legally incorrect. *In addition,* Mr. Shaw was not even eligible for Social Security benefits at the time of his death, *and* he could not qualify thereafter.

Revised: Plaintiff was factually and legally incorrect *for two reasons. First,* Mr. Shaw was not eligible for Social Security benefits at the time of his death. *Second,* Mr. Shaw could not qualify after his death.

2. *At the outset*, the search was made illegally because the officers had four days in which to acquire a search warrant and made no attempt to do so.

(Does "at the outset" mean "to begin this argument" or "at the beginning of the event?")

Revised: The search was illegal: the officers had four days in which to acquire a search warrant and made no attempt to do so.

3. He could not validly dispose of community property in the will *so that* part of the will is not valid.

Revised: Because he could not validly dispose of community property in the will, part of the will is not valid.

(f) Variety in Transitional Words

The general rule that the same word should be used to refer to the same thing can be overlooked when you are choosing transitions. If you use the word "however" or "therefore" six times in a paragraph, the reader will find it irritating, distracting, and finally meaningless. Here, a sense of variety and elegance may prevail over consistency in word choice. The lists below are meant to provide the legal writer with alternative transitional words and phrases. Selecting a precise transition is entirely a matter of context. Each of the following transitions will work well in some contexts but not in others.

Common Transitional Words And Phrases

Introducing

under these circumstances	in the first place
in order to	the first reason
to a certain extent	primarily
initially, first	viewed broadly
to begin, to begin with	in general

Concluding

to conclude
to sum up, in sum
in summary
to summarize
in review
to review
finally
up to this point
thus

therefore
consequently
as a result
eventually
in short
in brief
in particular
on the whole
as we have seen

Restating

that is
to clarify
in other words
in simpler terms
to simplify
more simply
to repeat

in brief
in short
in particular
on the whole
to put it differently
to be sure
as noted

Exemplifying

for example
for instance
to illustrate
that is
as an illustration

specifically
in particular
incidentally
namely

Emphasizing

of course
to be sure
indeed
in fact
as such
in effect
certainly
even, even so
nonetheless
in other words

after all
above all
actually
still
especially
at least
normally
notably
and rightly so
not only ... but also

Contrasting

however	in contrast
but	nonetheless
as the same time	rather
nevertheless	in opposition to
on the contrary	opposing
contrary to	although
on the other hand	in place of
yet	conversely
and yet	actually
though	despite
alternatively	in spite of
provided that	regardless
still	instead
unlike x	notwithstanding
otherwise	even so
by contrast	even though
although this may be true	
actually	

Adding or Amplifying

again	in other words
first, second, third	equally important
once again	of equal importance
further	incidentally
furthermore	nor
moreover	analogously
too	that is
additionally	provided that
similarly	alternatively
also	in the same vein
besides	after all
beyond this	a further reason

Comparing

similarly	by analogy
in like form, manner	analogously

likewise   in the same way

Sequencing

first, second, third
finally   in the first place
last
initially   soon
next   after
then

Cause and Effect

therefore   since
then   because
thus   for this purpose
as a result   to this end
hence   thereupon
accordingly   provided that
consequently   in effect
in consequence

Time or Place

above   later, lately
below   initially
beyond   eventually
simultaneously   meanwhile
subsequently   since
this time   more recently
until now   adjacent to
hitherto   opposite to
elsewhere   at length
formerly   ultimately
afterwards   shortly
earlier   thereafter

Alternatives for Overworked Transitions

Therefore   *And, In addition*
then   again
thus   further

hence
accordingly
as a result
consequently
besides
likewise
However, but
nevertheless
on the contrary
contrarily
on the other hand
yet
still
nonetheless
by contrast

furthermore
moreover
also
too
similarly

CHAPTER 4
SENTENCE DESIGN

§ 4.1 INTRODUCTION

This chapter offers suggestions for writing clear sentences. After the basic principles of sentence construction are explained, several techniques for enhancing readability are described, useful sentence patterns are illustrated, and sentence structures that commonly give rise to ambiguities are pointed out.

The principles of sentences construction are few and simple. First, begin a sentence with its subject, if you can. Second, place the verb close to the subject. Third, place the object close to the verb. Fourth, place modifiers next to things they modify. Finally, end the sentence swiftly.

§ 4.2 PRINCIPLES OF SENTENCE CONSTRUCTION

(a) Begin Sentences With Significant Words or Phrases

(1) Open a Sentence With its Subject

The reader expects the subject to come first. If it does not, then the reader must remember all the words that precede the subject until the subject appears. Nonlegal professional writers place something before the subject in only 25 percent of their sentences. Legal writers do so 50 percent of the time, sometimes more often. Try to limit the number of nonsubject sentence openers that you use.

> *Example of a Confusing Nonsubject Sentence Opener:* Regarding the plaintiff's situation, it would be no clarification to state simply that Case A is or is not consistent with Case B.

> *Revised:* The plaintiff's situation is not clarified by stating that Case A is or is not consistent with Case B.

If you do begin a sentence with something other than its subject, use words or phrases that set the stage for the subject-verb unit to follow. Successful nonlegal professional writers limit their nonsubject sentence openers to adverbial phrases and clauses, that is, to words or phrases that establish time, place, cause, and condition. Readers easily identify adverbial ideas as stage setting information and easily remember such ideas until the subject appears.

(2) *Place Transitional Words Near the Subject*

Readers expect to find transitional words somewhere in the first part of a sentence. Such words or phrases as "on the other hand" and "in a recent Supreme Court decision" may be used to open sentences or may be placed immediately after the subject. Although transitions are important, the subject of any sentence is generally more important. Thus, many writers prefer to place transitional elements after the subject. For example, rather than opening with "On the other hand, the proponents of the second view read the statute literally," the writer may place the subject first: "The proponents of the second view, on the other hand, read the statute literally." This places initial emphasis on the subject, "proponents," and final emphasis on the way in which the proponents read the statute, "literally."

(3) Do Not Routinely Open Sentences With Full Citations

Avoid the habitual use of a full citation as a sentence opener. The writer should spare the reader from having to comprehend or skip over a full citation in order to arrive at the point of a sentence. Whenever possible, place a full citation at the end of a sentence, preferably in a separate citation sentence, as demonstrated below:

Awkward opening: In *Kosters v. Seven–Up Co.,* 595 F.2d 347 (6th Cir.1979), the court held that a franchiser was liable for breach of warranty to an ultimate consumer who was injured by a defective product.

Revised: A franchiser has been held liable for breach of warranty to an ultimate consumer who was injured by a defective product. *Kosters v. Seven–Up Co.,* 595 F.2d 347 (6th Cir.1979).

The separate sentence citation is permissible if the cited authority supports or contradicts the full statement in the preceding sentence. If the cited authority supports or contradicts only part of the statement in the sentence, the citation must follow that part of the sentence.

A franchiser has been held liable to an ultimate consumer for breach of warranty, *Kosters v. Seven Up Co.,* 595 F.2d 347 (6th Cir.1979), but a licensor of personal property has been held not liable on warranty grounds, *Shaw v. Fairyland at Harvey's Inc.,* 26 App.Div.2d 576, 271 N.Y.S.2d 70 (1966).

If the writer wishes to emphasize a case name or other authority for which the citation has not yet been given, then the case citation may begin the sentence. For example, *"Buckley v. Valeo,* 424 U.S. 1 (1976), is the leading case on federal regulation of campaign spending." Even where a case is being emphasized, however, the complete citation may be placed last to improve readability: "The leading case on federal regulation of campaign spending is *Buckley v. Valeo*, 424 U.S. 1 (1976)."

When deciding whether to place a full citation first or last, ask yourself if the reader will need that information before reading the subject-verb unit. If not, then the citation will be a visual obstacle for the reader.

Shortened citation forms do not create such an obstacle, for example, " 'Outrageous conduct,' 316 U.S. at 7, was the court's characterization of the law officer's treatment of the defendant." Shortened names of cases or other authorities may serve as helpful transitional elements. The shortened citation or case name may be placed first in the sentence, or it may be placed after the subject as follows:

The Court in *Buckley* circumscribes federal regulation of campaign spending.

(b) **Keep Subject and Verb Close Together**

Subject and verb should be kept as close together as possible. As English speakers, we understand the subject and verb only as a unit, that is, neither subject nor verb is fully processed until the other is discovered. Keep verbs and objects close together for the same reason.

If a subject and verb (or a verb and object) must be separated, then they should be separated by no more than ten words. This seemingly arbitrary rule requires an explanation. Our short-term memory accurate holds seven items, for example, telephone numbers, physical objects such as cars or pedestrians in an intersection, decimal digits, and monosyllabic words. (This mnemonic limit is sometimes referred to as the Magical Number Seven, Plus or Minus Two.) Thus, for each group of seven words in a sentence, there must be what is called "closure"; that is, the words must form a self-enclosed unit, for example (i) a subject with modifiers ("the case on appeal"), (ii) phrases ("in other words"), and (iii) clauses ("that the court will recognize").

We read and remember in segments. Social security numbers and telephone numbers are segmented to help us remember them. In the same way, sentences must be segmented (have frequent closure) if the reader is to understand on first reading. In reality, lawyers and law students are compelled to read sentences containing segments of a dozen words or more. Each word in such a segment must be held individually in the short-term memory until the segment is closed. If closure is delayed too long, the reader forgets the initial words in the segment and so must reread.

Perhaps because lawyers have daily practice with long segments or words, they appear to have an ability to hold more than seven items in the short-term memory (or at least they tolerate the strain). The legal writer may thus wish to observe the Magical Number limit when writing for lay readers and to extend it slightly when writing for legally trained readers. Ten words is a reasonable limit for the legal writer to observe when writing for other lawyers. Longer gaps are not "wrong," of course; they simply compel the reader to reread the sentence.

> *Subject and Verb Too Far Apart: Continuation* [S] of partnership upon retirement, death, or bankruptcy of a partner and *disposition of* [S$_2$] the partnership interests of the retiring, deceased, or bankrupt partner *should be* [V] subject to majority vote.

> *Revision that Keeps Subject and Verb Together: Continuation* [S$_1$] of partnership *should* also *be* [V$_1$] subject to majority vote after any partner retires, dies, or suffers bankruptcy. At that time, *disposition of partnership interests* [S$_s$] *should* also *be* [V$_s$] subject to majority vote.

Subject and Verb may be moved closer together in various ways, as in these two additional revisions of the first sentence:

1. If a partner retires, dies, or suffers bankruptcy, *continuation* [S$_1$] of partnership *should be* [V$_1$] subject to majority vote.

2. After the retirement, death, or bankruptcy of
    a partner, *continuation* [S_1] of partnership
    should be [V_1] subject to majority vote.

(c) Use Subject–Verb–Object Pattern

Nearly all sentences should be written in the
active voice, that is, following the Subject–Verb–
Object pattern. This is the pattern most readily
comprehended by English speakers. When the doer
of an action is in the Subject position (and the
receiver of an action is in the Object position), the
sentence is active and thus most forceful: "Defendant's car hit the plaintiff's fence." When the doer
of an action is moved to the Object position and the
receiver of an action is moved to the Subject position (that is, Subject and Object are reversed), the
sentence is passive and tends to lose forcefulness.
"The plaintiff's fence was hit by the defendant's
car."

When deciding whether to use active or passive
voice, ask yourself, first, whether the reader needs
to know the subject and, second, whether you want
the reader to know the subject. If the answer to
either question is affirmative, then use the active
voice. If the answer is negative, use the passive.

The passive voice is useful if you do not know the
subject or if you wish to:

(i) emphasize what was done rather than who did
     it:

     The defendant's car was crushed.

(ii) vary sentence structure:

The clerk reviewed the record. The judge studied the record and the briefs. Afterward they agreed that *the record had been misread by* both counsel.

(iii) depersonalize tone by making acts anonymous:

The records were misplaced.

(iv) emphasize facts:

Drawers had been pulled out, clothes were strewn about the floor, even valuable jewelry had been scattered over the dresser top. These facts, found by the lower court, emphasize the reckless nature of the sheriff's search.

(d) Keep Related Parts of the Sentence Together

(1) Introduction

The most common result of not keeping related words together is the misplaced modifier. A misplaced modifier is a word, phrase, or clause that appears to modify the wrong thing. Modifiers should be placed next to the word or words that they modify. Misplaced modifiers can occur at any point in a sentence and often result in ambiguity.

Keep this general rule in mind: If a reader must reread a sentence in order to determine what modifies what, then the sentence is poorly constructed and should be rewritten. A charitable reader will be able to sort out most ambiguous modifiers. The legal writer cannot, however, rely on the charity of legal readers. If any two lawyers are asked the meaning of a sentence with an ambiguous modifier, they may give the same interpretation if they consider the sentence in the abstract. Their answers may differ, however, if they must consider the sentence from the viewpoints of clients with conflicting interests.

In a recent case, for example, a $55,000 judgment rested on the interpretation of an allegedly misplaced word. The disputed word, which cost the losing side the full $55,000, was "available": "The scour protection fill may be pit-run gravel available in natural position on shore at the project site or other suitable material acceptable to the engineer." The question was whether the fill "may be available" or whether pit-run gravel was available and might be used as fill. Depending on the drafter's intent, the sentence should have been written either of two ways:

The fill may or may not be available in natural position.

The pit-run gravel that is available may be used as fill.

(2) *Avoid Misplaced Modifiers at the Beginning of a Sentence*

1. *Confusing:* By doing so, the security interest will not survive bankruptcy. (Who is "doing so"? Not the "security interest.")

Clear: If we do so, the security interest will not survive bankruptcy.

2. *Confusing:* As your lawyer, the dog must be leashed.

Clear: As your lawyer, I advise you to leash your dog.

(3) *Avoid Misplaced Modifiers in the Middle of a Sentence*

Modifying words or phrases may "squint," that is, look both ways, in the middle of a sentence.

Adverbs like "well," "only," "often," and "both" are particularly troublesome in mid-sentence.

1.   A lawyer who can write *well* deserves her fee. (Does any lawyer who can write deserve her fee? Or do only those who write *well* deserve it?)

Revised by rephrasing: A lawyer who is a skilled writer deserves her fee.

2.   A contractor who fails to complete construction on time often cannot be made to pay a penalty. (If a contractor fails often, then he cannot be made to pay? Or is it often the case that contractors who fail to complete construction on time cannot be made to pay?)

Revise by moving "often" or by substituting "cannot always be made to pay."

3.   The decision favors *both* the positions taken in *Copra* and *Coldewey*. (Both positions taken in each case? One position taken in both cases? Two distinct positions, one in each case? More than one position taken in each case?)

Revise by writing out in full.

(4) Avoid Split Infinitives

Infinitives should be split only if ambiguity or awkwardness results from leaving them intact.

Writers sometimes place modifiers inside an infinitive ("to *unduly* influence," "to *specifically* perform") to avoid such ambiguous sentences as these:

The court imposed new requirements *strictly to regulate* interstate sales of toxic sprays.

The court imposed new requirements *to regulate strictly* interstate sales of toxic sprays.

If the adverb "strictly" is not to modify either "imposed" (Meaning "imposed in a strict way") or "interstate" (Meaning "exclusively interstate"), then the infinitive "to regulate" must be split:

The court imposed new requirements *to strictly regulate* interstate sales of toxic sprays.

Sentences that require a split infinitive, like the above example, are relatively few. A simple revision will usually eliminate the potential ambiguity without the need for splitting the infinitive.

Unnecessarily Split Infinitive: Judicial discretion allows the court to *both fulfill* its role as parens patriae to the child and *to consider fully* the rights of the child.

Revised: Judicial discretion allows the court *both to fulfill* its role as parens patriae to the child and *to consider fully* the rights of the child.

(5) *Avoid Ambiguous Modifiers at the End of a Sentence*

Avoid unwanted ambiguity stemming from ambiguous modifiers at the end.

1. *Confusing*: The court reviewed the 1965 Act in its dicta, changing the requirements for good faith bargaining. (Dicta changes? The Act changes? The Court changes?)

Clear: In its dicta, the Court reviewed the 1965 Act, which changes the requirements for good faith bargaining. (The Act changes.)

2. *Confusing*: "Affiliate of the Partnership of the General Partners" does not include a Person who is a Partner in a partnership with the Partnership or with the General Partners or their affiliates, *which*

person is not otherwise an Affiliate of the Partnership of the General Partners. (Which person?)

(e) End Sentences Swiftly and Effectively

As soon as you have completed a subject-verb unit, consider ending the sentence. Continue to write another subject-verb unit in the same sentence only if ideas are so closely related that they must be joined.

(1) Put Significant Words or Phrases in the Final Position

The two "emphatic positions" in a sentence are the beginning and the end. Be certain that the words you place in these two emphatic positions deserve to be there.

Unemphatic: We recommend that the Company discuss with us further its plans for obtaining outside investment *in the future.*

Revised: We recommend that the Company discuss with us further its plans for obtaining future *outside investment.*

(2) Avoid Prepositional Phrases in the Final Position

Final prepositional phrases are usually weak and sometimes ambiguous.

Rhetorically Weak and Ambiguous Series of Prepositions: Also enclosed is a letter I prepared *in* response *to* a request *for* explanation *of* certain features *of* an individual employment contract *for* a plant supervisor.

Revised: Also enclosed is a letter I prepared for a plant supervisor to explain certain features of an individual employment contract.

Or: Also enclosed is a letter I prepared to explain certain features of a plant supervisor's individual employment contract.

§ 4.3 TECHNIQUES TO ENHANCE READABILITY

(a) Use Short and Medium–Length Sentences

The best professional prose on complex or technical subjects averages 20 words per sentence. For legal writers, this average is slightly higher (20 to 25 words per sentence). Although a variety of sentence lengths is important to avoid monotony (which actually retards comprehension), even the longer sentences normally should not exceed 35 words.

To determine your average number of words per sentence, take a representative sample of your prose (at least 250 words) and count the words. Count as single words hyphenated words, abbreviations, numbers, and case names. Omit citation sentences from the count. In citations within a sentence, consider as single words the case name, the reported citation, and the date. Next count the number of sentences and divide for the average. If it is greater than 25, you should concentrate on writing shorter sentences. Using the same writing sample, check for variety in sentence lengths: sentences should vary from short to long without monotony in length or pattern of occurrence. There should be some short, some medium, and some long, but not in any discernible order.

(b) Make One Point Per Sentence

Two related ideas may be joined by a semicolon without significantly lessening readability. In general, however, keep separate thoughts in separate sentences.

(c) Make Sentences Affirmative, Not Negative

We understand affirmative statements more quickly and easily than negative ones. In studies of the effects of language on the mind, researchers have found that affirmative statements are psychologically more linear than negative ones. With negative statements, we must first understand the affirmative sense, then negate it. This is analogous to understanding another language by first translating it into one's own. Avoid these nearly incomprehensible combinations: "not otherwise," "never unless," "none unless," "never otherwise," and so forth.

Negative Sentence: The Plaintiff must not be prevented from bringing a suit.

Affirmative Revision: The Plaintiff must be allowed to bring a suit.

Confusing Negative Words or Ideas:

1. Contrary to opposing counsel's denial, the facts dispose of the primary defense.

Revised: The facts contradict the primary defense raised by counsel for the defendant.

2. Not only is there no evidence that Mr. Jones relied upon the booklet, but also, even if he had, it would not change the outcome of this case.

Revised: Even if Mr. Jones had relied upon the booklet (and evidence is lacking), the outcome would remain the same.

(d) Use Parallelism and Balance in Sentence Structures

Parallelism is similarity of structure, that is, repetition of like words in the same order, for example, "He came, he saw, he conquered." A reader will be better able to absorb new information if parallel structures are used because the structure will be "transparent." That is, only the meaning of the words themselves must be processed, not a new structure. Compare this nonparallel structure with the above version: "After he came, he looked and then conquered."

Parallel structure is particularly helpful in a sentence containing multiple subjects, verbs, or objects. Legal writers frequently use such compound structures, which tend to be confusing unless they are given parallel structure. If a compound structure must be used, keep word order and parts of speech the same when possible, for example, "We agreed *to exchange documents* and *to share expenses*."

Balanced structure refers to groupings of words which are of roughly the same length. Such structures need not be worded similarly. They need only "sound" rhythmical to the reader's ear. Rhythmic patterns within sentences, as well as a rhythmic variation of sentences within paragraphs, increase readability in two ways. First, rhythmic patterns allow the reader's mind to anticipate how much attention will be required for each syllable to come. This makes reading easier. In the same way, music in which sound patters are rhythmic is easier to listen to than music in which every note comes as a surprise. When there is a discernible melody, we can prepare for what is to come. Thus we process what *does* come more quickly.

Effective use of parallelism and balance also lends emphasis and allows density (greater detail) without loss of readability.

Effective Use of Parallelism and Balance:

The conduct of the officers in *searching Mr. Smiley, seizing his property*, and *arresting him* is exactly the type of conduct the fourth amendment was designed to prevent.

Revision for Parallelism:

Without Parallelism: The Company should place on its stock certificates a disclaimer and should make a notation in its stock records.

Revised: The Company should place a disclaimer on its stock certificates and make a notation on its stock records.

(e) Provide Extra Structural Clues

(1) Include Essential "That"

Use of the word "that" is frequently essential to the correct reading of a sentence. It is not an "extra" clue in these instances, but rather an essential structural clue. The italicized phrases or clauses in the following examples may be misread as discrete units. Without the essential structural clue, the reader may have to reread these sentences for initial comprehension.

1.   The complainant has the burden of *proving the rates* violate the statute. (The reader wonders initially how the complainant will "prove rates.")

Revised: The complainant has the burden of proving *that* the rates violate the statute.

2.   When a manufacturer advertises his product, *he knows his acts,* whether intended or not, may have consequences in another state. (The initial reading may be that a manufacturer "knows his acts," which is not the point.)

Revised: When a manufacturer advertises his products, he knows *that* his acts, whether intended or not, may have consequences in another state.

(2) *Repeat Some Structure Words to Improve Readability*

1.   I am aware that the securities are not being registered under the federal Securities Act of 1933 or any state securities laws, pursuant to exemptions from registration.

Revised: I am aware that the securities are not being registered under the federal Securities Act of 1933 or *under* any state securities laws, pursuant to exemptions from registration.

2.   We recommend that the Company discuss with us its plans for obtaining future outside investment and granting stock options.

Revised: We recommend that the Company discuss with us its plans for obtaining future outside investment and *for* granting stock options.

§ 4.4 USEFUL SENTENCE PATTERNS FOR LEGAL WRITING

(a) Basic Sentence Types

Of the three basic sentence types (simple, compound, and complex), simple and complex should dominate legal writing.

Most sentences should be simple in structure, that is, one subject-verb unit. Use an occasional four-to-six word sentence for emphasis. The simple sentence is the pattern best suited for expressing one idea at a time, something all legal writers should attempt to do.

Simple: Subject (S)   +   Verb(V)
             (The boat   leaks.)

If two ideas must be included in the same sentence, the complex sentence pattern may be more economical than the compound.

   Complex:

   (i) $S + V$, Subordinating Conjunction $S + V$
            (The boat did not sink, even though it leaks.)

   (ii) Subordinating Conjunction $S + V$, $S + V$
            (Even though the boat leaks, it did not sink.)

Subordinating conjunctions include:

after	inasmuch as	until
although	in order that	when
as	in that	whenever
as if	provided	where
because	since	wherever
before	so that	whether
how	that	while
if	unless	

Compound:

(i) S + V, Coordinating Conjunction S + V
      (The boat did not sink, but it leaks.)

(ii) S + V; S + V
      (The boat leaks; it did not sink.)

Coordinating conjunctions include:

and	for	or
but	nor	yet

(iii) S + V; Conjunctive Adverb, S + V
      (The boat leaks; however, it did not sink.)

(iv) S, Conjunctive Adverb, V; S + V
      (The boat, however, did not sink; it simply leaks.)

Conjunctive adverbs include:

also	in fine	so
as a result	likewise	still
besides	moreover	therefore
consequently	nevertheless	thus
henceforth	notwithstanding	yet
however	otherwise	

The complex pattern is more efficient than the compound because it establishes a logical and a hierarchical relationship between two ideas. Because a subordinating conjunction subordinates one subject-verb unit to another, the relative importance of the two ideas in a complex sentence is automatically reflected by the sentence structure. Compare the relative importance of the two ideas (subject-verb units) in the following sentences:

1. *Compound Sentence Pattern*: The damages have exceeded the original estimates by 55%, and Mr. Baggins is unable to settle this case.

Complex Sentence Pattern: Because the damages have exceeded the original estimates by 55%, Mr. Baggins is unable to settle this case.

In the complex sentence, emphasis falls on Mr. Baggins' inability to settle the case. In the compound sentence, the uninformative word "and" does nothing more than establish a loose connection, rather like a "plus" in addition. It carries no other information about the relationship between the clauses it joins.

2. *Compound:* The wage differential has existed since the initial hiring of the coaches, so it would be very difficult for the school district to assert seniority as the basis for that differential.

Complex: Since the wage differential existed when the coaches were initially hired, it would be very difficult for the school district to assert seniority as the basis for that differential.

(b) Useful Patterns: "If ... Then"

An "If ... then" sentence pattern may be used to establish a condition, to describe a complex cause-and-effect situation, or to detail a sequence of events. This pattern permits complexity without a wide separation of subject and verb. Both the "if-clause" and the "then-clause" contain their own subject-verb units, making them easier for the reader to grasp. A "When ... then" structure works identically, but has a slightly different meaning. The word "then" need not be included in the sentence, although it does assist the reader.

Ordinarily, use no more than two "if-clauses" in a sentence. A succession of "if-clauses" leading to a final "then-clause" will be hard to comprehend on one reading. You should indent and enumerate if more than two "if-clauses" are needed before a "then-clause" can follow.

1. *Confusing:* We will not discuss a settlement with you without the manager asking her bookkeeper to compile a final statement covering all construction

costs and allowing Sam Perkins to look at the books and satisfy himself that things were done properly.

Revised: If the manager will ask her bookkeeper to compile a final statement covering all construction costs and if Sam Perkins can look at the books and satisfy himself that things were done properly, then we will discuss a settlement.

2. *Confusing:* We ask that this be done and that the management problem be openly and honestly discussed in order that the matter be settled amicably and at the least possible expense.

Revised: If this is done and the management problem is openly and honestly discussed, then the matter could be settled amicably at the lease possible expense.

In the first example, the second modifier "allowing" is too far from the noun it modifies ("manager") for rapid comprehension. The reader must reread the sentence. An "if ... then" structure eliminates this problem. In the second example, the double object and the lengthy clause beginning "in order that" extend the sentence beyond the length comfortable for most readers.

(c) Useful Patterns: Stating a Rule and Exception

If a rule and an exception occur in the same sentence, the rule should be stated first. The reader will not understand the exception fully or remember it well without the rule already in mind. The best way to handle rules, exceptions, and conditions is to give each its own sentence, for example, "As a general rule.... An exception, however, is...."

The court has consistently recognized an absolute immunity for statements made in judicial proceedings. If a person has suffered special injury in such proceedings, however, the court has recognized an exception to that immunity by approving an action for malicious prosecution.

(d) Useful Patterns: Reversal of Direct Object and Prepositional Phrases

When the direct object is longer and more detailed than a prepositional phrase that modifies the verb, the prepositional phrase may be placed first after the verb. This gives the reader a better chance of remembering the verb while reading both the direct object and the prepositional phrase.

Confusing: Cynthia Williams of Browning Associates transferred [V] the property [DO] that had been held in trust for twenty-five years to George Berry [PP].

Clear: Cynthia Williams of Browning Associates transferred [V] to George Berry [PP] the property [DO] that had been held in trust for twenty-five years.

(e) Useful Patterns: Periodic Sentence

In the periodic sentence, the main thought is not completed until the end of the sentence, thus creating suspense and taking full advantage of the final emphatic position.

1.   If the individual arrested is diagnosed as an alcoholic, early commitment for effective treatment, either on a voluntary or involuntary basis, is essential.

2.   When you consider the chaos that ensued, it is remarkable that anyone—witnesses, victims, or defendant—can recall the details of the automobile collision.

To achieve its effect, the periodic sentence is often opened with "it" or "there" or "the fact that." These pronouns or other "place-fillers" stand in for the subject (itself reserved for a later or final position in the sentence). Although this sentence pattern can be effective if used sparingly, it is sometimes overused in legal writing, especially in argument. Use it with care and only for special emphasis.

§ 4.5 PRINCIPLES FOR AVOIDING AMBIGUOUS OR CONFUSING SENTENCES

(a) Avoid the "Not ... Because" Sentence Pattern

If the word "not" comes before the word "because" in a sentence, the sentence may be ambiguous. It will frequently be hard to read, whether or not it is ambiguous. The reader may not know whether you mean "Not because of this, but rather because of that" or whether you mean "Not so, and for this reason."

1. *Confusing*: The fact that no mention of Defendant was made in the will does not preclude her because she is his legal heir. (Because she is his heir, lack of mention will not preclude her? Or does it preclude her not because she is his heir but rather because of something else?)

Clear: Because she is his legal heir, the absence of a mention of her in the will does not preclude her.

2. *Confusing*: The threshold requirement of a common core of tasks is not met because of the inherent

differences between coaching baseball and coaching tennis. (Requirement is not met because of differences but rather because of something else? Or differences prevent the requirement from being met?)

Clear: Because there are inherent differences between coaching baseball and coaching tennis, the threshold requirement of a common core of tasks is not met.

(b) Avoid Ambiguous Prepositional Phrases

(1) *Introduction*

Prepositional phrases present many challenges to the legal writer. They are easily misplaced and thus often misread. Ambiguities frequently result from strings of prepositional phrases inside a sentence and from prepositional phrases beginning with the word "with" at the end of a sentence.

(2) *Place Prepositional Phrases Next to What They Modify*

Ambiguous: Plaintiff pleads that the letter was found to be insufficient in Paragraph IV of his complaint. (In Paragraph IV, the letter was insufficient?)

Precise: Plaintiff pleads, in Paragraph IV of his complaint, that the letter was found to be insufficient.

(3) *Avoid Strings of Prepositional Phrases*

Multiple prepositional phrases may be ambiguous, especially at the end of a sentence. The following sentence, for example, may be read to mean a number of things, including the idea that justice is based on the individual's capacity for self-government.

The continued existence of a free and democratic society depends upon recognition of the concept that justice is based upon respect for the dignity of the individual and his capacity through reason for enlightened self-government within the meaning of the rule of law.

(4) Beware of Adjacent Prepositional Phrases

Ambiguous: They examined every figure in the account in defendant's handwriting. (Is the entire account in defendant's handwriting or just some of the figures?)

Precise: They examined every figure that defendant had written in the account.

(5) Beware of "With" and "Without" Phrases in Final Position

These phrases are sometimes ambiguous at the end of a sentence. Substitute more precise words.

Ambiguous structure: Noun + Verb + Object + with + Noun

1. *Ambiguous*: Our client will finance the contract with expenses. (Client will finance using expenses?)

Precise: Our client will finance the contract and the expenses.

2. *Ambiguous*: Several courts have found jurisdiction proper for a private complainant without any interpretation of the statute.

Precise: Without interpreting the statute, several courts have found jurisdiction proper for a private complainant.

(c) Avoid Sentences Beginning With Relative Pronouns

Sentences beginning with "who," "which," or "that" will probably require rereading unless they are short.

1. *That* the group associated for the sole purpose of committing crimes constitutes a pattern of racketeering activity.

Revised: A pattern of racketeering is established because the group associated for the sole purpose of committing crimes.

2. *Which* decision the court will uphold is, given the balance of authority, impossible accurately to predict.

Revised: Because the decisions are of equal weight, it is impossible to predict which the court will uphold.

3. *Which expert* the opposing counsel uses as a witness will determine the cross-examination strategy we will adopt.

Revised: Our cross-examination strategy will depend on *which* expert opposing counsel uses as a witness.

§ 4.6   SENTENCE REVISION

(a) A Simple Method for Revising Troublesome Sentences

(1) First, Lift Main Subject, Verb, and Object From the Sentence

Reread each unsatisfactory sentence quickly to find the subject, verb, and object, and "lift" them from the rest of the sentence. The following sentence, for example, needs revision:

Having determined, as it has, that the protection of the public's interest in the shorelines, in water quality, in air quality, and in other subjects, requires compliance with a carefully drawn statutory scheme, the legislature is not entitled to single out one specific activity or category of project for exception from the scheme in that its motive is clearly to sacrifice environment protection to speeding up the licensing process.

Main Subject: "legislature"

Main Verb Phrase: "is not entitled to single out"

Objects: "one activity," "category"

If the key idea is "legislature is not entitled to single out one activity or category," then the revision should begin with that key idea. The idea should not be buried in the middle of the sentence, but should instead appear in a separate sentence.

Revised: The legislature is not entitled to single out one activity or category for exception from the statutory scheme. (The rest of the example is revised below.)

(2) Second, Remove Imprecise Subject–Verb Combinations

Fuzzy sentences are often the result of an imprecise subject-verb combination. This imprecision, hidden by the rest of the sentence, becomes evident when the subject and verb are lifted from the rest of the sentence.

Initial subject and verb from above example:

[T]he *protection* ... *requires* compliance.

This fuzzy notion, that "protection" can somehow "require" something, obscures the thought in the sentence. The subject, or the "who" in the sentence, should be the legislature: "the legislature requires compliance in order to protect the public's interest."

(3) Third, Revise for Subject–Verb–Object Order

After you have isolated the subject and verb, consider moving the subject to the beginning of the sentence. This often means relocating an initial phrase or clause, such as the clause in (1) above: "Having determined, as it has, that the protection of the public's interest in the shorelines, in water quality, in air quality, and in other subjects, requires compliance with a carefully drawn statutory scheme." This 33–word introductory clause should be converted to a sentence of its own, again by first locating the subject(s) and verb(s) and then by revising:

Legislature [S] *has determined* [V] (that) *protection* [S$_2$] *requires* [V$_2$] *compliance* [O$_2$].

Revised: The legislature has determined that compliance with a carefully drawn statutory scheme is required for protection of the public's interest in the shorelines, in water quality, in air quality, and in other subjects.

Thus, the original long sentence has been revised by several simple procedures, into three shorter sentences:

Revised: The legislature has determined that compliance with a carefully drawn statutory scheme is required for protection of the public's interest in the shorelines, in water quality, in air quality, and in other subjects. Having done so, the legislature is not entitled to single out one activity or category for exception from the statutory scheme. The legislature's motive for making such exceptions is to speed up the licensing process at the expense of environmental protection.

(b) Simple Techniques for Shortening Sentences

(1) Introduction

Long sentences may be broken into several shorter ones as demonstrated below by (i) eliminating unnecessary words, (ii) converting long sentences to simpler, shorter ones, and (iii) transferring parenthetical expressions to another sentence.

(2) Eliminate Unnecessary Words

The legal writer must learn to distinguish between redundancy and helpful repetition of words or ideas. Do not, for example, eliminate structural clues, as described in a preceding section. Do, however, eliminate such redundancies as "basic fundamentals" or "with lucid clarity."

If time permits, reread each word and ask yourself, "Do I need this word? Will anything significant be lost if I take it out?" If you do this, you will begin to form the habit of writing concisely. Occasionally, words that could be left out improve the rhythm of a sentence or paragraph. Improved sound or rhythm is, however, no excuse for using flabby intensifiers like "very" and "pretty much." When excess is removed, emphasis occurs naturally and rhythm is improved.

Avoid writing sentences beginning with an unnecessary "It . . . that" structure.

1.   *Wordy*: It is the theory that lends itself ...

Concise: The theory lends itself ...

2.   *Wordy*: It must be noted, however, that the authority ...

Concise: Note, however, that the authority ...

3.   *Wordy*: It can be said with certainty, moreover, that a structural violation will be recognized by all courts.

Concise: Moreover, a structural violation will certainly be recognized by all courts.

4.   *Wordy*: Again, it should be emphasized that it is doubtful that a naked allegation of mismanagement of funds by the trustees would confer jurisdiction.

Concise: A naked allegation of mismanagement of funds by the trustees would probably not confer jurisdiction.

5.   *Wordy*: It is unlikely that one who fails to make a case of wage discrimination under the Equal Pay Act would prevail with the same claim under Title VII.

Concise: One who fails to make a case of wage discrimination under the Equal Pay Act is not likely to prevail with the same claim under Title VII.

Also avoid sentences beginning with an "In that the" structure, and avoid internal clauses beginning with "in that." These are clumsy, difficult to read, and verbose.

Wordy: In that the witness is also an interested party, his testimony is suspect.

Concise: The witness's testimony is suspect because he is an interested party.

Or: Because he is an interested party, the witness's testimony is suspect.

(3) Convert Long Compound Sentences to Shorter Sentences

Replace "and," "but," "or," "nor," and "for" with a period.

If he was not insured on reaching the age of 65, he does not become insured by reason of any insurable employment which he takes up later, and the special contributions which are payable under the Act only by his employer, in respect of such employment, do not give him any title to health insurance benefits or pension, and moreover a man is not at liberty to pay any contributions on his own account as a voluntary contributor for any period after his 65th birthday.

Revised: If he was not insured at age 65, he does not become insured by reason of any insurable employment that he takes up later. The special contributions that are payable under the Act only by his employer, in respect of such employment, do not give him any title to health insurance benefits or pension. Moreover, a man is not at liberty to pay any contributions on his own account as a voluntary contributor for any period after his 65th birthday.

(4) Transfer Internal Clauses or Parenthetical Expressions to Another Sentence

Too Long: The district court in Maryland in a recent case stated that the EEOC's policy of sending right-to-sue letters immediately after the filing of the charge, *if the regional director ascertains that the charge cannot be investigated within 180 days*, was "inconsistent with an obvious congressional intent."

Revised: The EEOC's policy is to send right-to-sue letters immediately after the filing of the charge, *if the regional director ascertains that the charge cannot be investigated within 180 days*. The district court in a recent case stated that the policy was "inconsistent with an obvious congressional intent."

(c) How to Acquire Efficient Revision Habits

Few legal writers have time to revise every sentence they write. Fewer still have time to follow each of the above suggestions every time they write. How can a legal writer, writing every day under pressure, acquire good revision habits?

The answer is to acquire them slowly, one by one. Take one suggestion for revision at a time, for example: "Use short sentences." Review the next piece you write for sentence length. Read each sentence, and shorten those that are too long. This may take an extra few minutes, but it will "program" your "mental computer" to be alert for overlong sentences. Repeat this for the next few pieces of writing. The human brain is a miraculous machine. It will absorb your new revision technique and incorporate it into your intuitive writing style.

Then select another tip or revision. For example, review for sentence openers. Revise so that most sentences open with their subjects. Repeat this for the next few pieces of writing. If your "computer" was well programmed for sentence length, then you will automatically be checking for that as well. A few days or weeks later, select a third strategy, for example, subject-verb distance. Review each sentence for that. Continue with this system until you have "programmed" a solution to each of the writing problems you have. This "programming" will require a small investment of time at first but will ultimately save time, both for you and for your readers.

Those revision practices that you select—those that suit your personal style—will become part of your intuitive behavior, both while writing and afterwards during revision. Once they become part of your intuitive writing behavior, you will writer faster and more effectively. For a complete analysis of your writing, see Chapter 7.

CHAPTER 5

LANGUAGE IN THE LEGAL SETTING

The most important matter is to identify the ideas ... but the choice of the word to express the idea is of almost equal importance. The expressions of one whose ideas are confused and uncertain will of necessity be equally confusing to others; but the effort to choose a word that will clearly convey an idea to others is of great assistance in clarifying to one self the idea that should be conveyed.

> — 3 *Corbin on Contracts* 7 (1960)

§ 5.1 INTRODUCTION

Correct usage of legal and nonlegal language is fundamental to clear writing, but in a given context there is seldom only one "correct" word choice. The introduction to language in this chapter is intended to help the legal writer make effective choices as well as correct choices. The introduction includes principles for word selection and a discussion of redundancy in legal writing. The chapter concludes with a glossary of words commonly misused in legal writing.

§ 5.2 PRINCIPLES FOR MAKING WORD CHOICES

To say precisely what we mean requires thought: first, we must identify what we mean, and, second, we must decide how best to express it. Many writers use the words that come automatically to mind without giving them further thought. These automatic word choices are not necessarily the best choices. The following principles will help you to make effective word choices rather than automatic word choices.

(a) Use Words in Their Literal Sense

A common source of imprecision in legal writing is personification, the giving of human qualities to abstractions or objects, for example, "cold-blooded decision." A related source of imprecision is metonymy, the substitution of an attributive or a suggestive word for the word identifying a person or thing, for example, "stage hand" for "stage worker." In some types of writing, this kind of imprecision may be acceptable; in legal writing, precision is essential.

1. *Imprecise*: The five points analyze the statute.

Precise: The court analyzes the statute in five points.

2. *Imprecise*: California has so held.

Precise: The California Court of Appeals has so held.

3. *Imprecise*: This Washington case so found.

Precise: The jury in this Washington case so found.

(b) Omit Archaic Legalisms

Archaic legalisms are words and phrases, such as "hereinafter," "heretofore," "aforesaid," "forthwith," "herein," "hereby," "for purposes hereof," "notwithstanding anything to the contrary herein," "so made," "by these presents," and "said." Not only are these words obstacles to the lay reader, but they are also imprecise and thus troublesome to the legal reader. For example, if the words "thereof" and "therefrom" are removed from the following sentence, it gains both clarity and readability:

> The following assets for administration under this Article 4, including the proceeds, investments and reinvestments *thereof*, and accumulated income *therefrom*, if any, shall constitute the "trust estate."

> *Revised:* The following assets for administration under Article 4, including the proceeds, investments, reinvestments, and accumulated income from the assets shall constitute the "trust estate."

Archaic legalisms may create the appearance of precision, thus obscuring ambiguities that might otherwise be recognized. For example, a question that has been frequently litigated is whether "herein" refers to the paragraph in which it is used, the section, or the whole document. Therefore, after removing the archaic language, consider whether you must add precise references to time, place, or subject matter.

(c) Use the Same Word to Refer to the Same Thing; Use Different Words to Refer to Different Things

Never attempt to improve style by introducing synonyms or other word variations that will create confusion or ambiguity. In the following sentences, the substitution of the word "prevailing" for the word "dominant" creates initial confusion: Is the author going to discuss two views?

> According to the *dominant view*, this article is applied to periodic meetings as well as to special meetings. The *prevailing view* is that Article 237 of the Commercial Code provides the right for minority shareholders to convene either type of meeting.

Similarly, from the following sentence can we know whether the author is discussing two or three forms of copyright?

> Although under the old Act *a common law copyright* existed in writings until they qualified for statutory protection, the *non-statutory copyright* was extinguished when the *statutory copyright* was created by publication or registration.

A corollary is to use different words when you mean different things. If the same word is used to mean different things, the reader will be at least momentarily confused.

1. In *case of* litigation in the present *case*, the accountant's testimony will be crucial.

2. In a sub*point* to the second argument, the court makes the *point* that intent should control.

3. As a final *consideration*, there was no discussion of the contractor's *consideration*.

4. Under our present system of criminal *sanctions*, legislative limits and judicial discretion *sanction* individualization of sentences.

(d) Use Simple, Familiar Words

When you have a choice between a short, familiar word, such as "call," and a longer, more elaborate word, such as "communicate," choose the shorter, simpler one. Simple words are understood more quickly. They require less reading and thinking time.

Simple Words	*Elaborate Counterparts*
after	subsequent to
before	prior to
begin, carry out	implement, effectuate
happen	eventuate, transpire
inform	apprise
make	render
sent	transmit
think	deem
think, see, regard	envisage

(e) Use Concrete Rather than Abstract Words

Concrete words such as "split decision" are easier to understand than abstractions such as "judicial dichotomy." Legal writers are likely to use abstract, overblown language in part because many of the cases that law students read during their first year reflect an older, overstuffed style that is all too easy to imitate. Legal writers must resist the old style.

Some common abstractions are simple words that can often be eliminated without loss of meaning for example, "type," "kind," "manner," "state," "area," "matter," "factor," "system," and "nature."

1. *The central thrust* of plaintiff's legal *position* is dependent on *matters* having to do with three decisions of the United States Supreme Court.

Revised: Plaintiff's argument for summary judgment depends on three United States Supreme Court decisions.

2.   The court may not abandon the traditional termination-at-will *manner* of analysis in order to apply a reasonableness *factor* in the *area* of non-employment contracts.

Revised: The court may not abandon the traditional termination-at-will analysis for non-employment contracts in order to apply the reasonableness analysis.

3.   The above arguments *are likely to encounter two problems due to* the particular *kind of facts* in this case. (Abstract subject-verb-object: arguments encounter problems.)

Revised: Our client's delay and abusive manner weaken the good faith argument in this case. ("Delay and abusive manner" make specific what "kind of facts" are referred to.)

(f) Use Words That Are Consistent in Tone

All words have connotation (overtones of meaning) as well as denotation (explicit meaning). Since connotation contributes to tone, the word choices in a particular piece of legal writing should have compatible connotations. Many briefs contain glaring inconsistencies in tone, as in the following excerpt from a fact statement:

A third-party park-sitter, unbeknownst to Plaintiff, contacted said Plaintiff's head with a wine bottle. Plaintiff now has two metal plates and twelve screws holding things together.

(g) Avoid Equivocations

Lawyers and law students often hesitate to make direct or dogmatic statements. To protect themselves or to reflect uncertainty, they use either equivocal or qualifying words that undermine their meaning. Typical words and phrases used in this way are: "it seems to indicate," "if practicable," "it would seem," "it may well be," and "it might be said that." If you are uncertain, state the reason for your uncertainty.

(h) Use Unqualified Nouns, Adjectives, and Verbs

Many writers add modifiers to intensify or buttress poorly chosen nouns, adjectives, and verbs. The right word ordinarily needs no bolstering. When the following modifiers are removed, emphasis falls naturally where it should: on the noun, adjective, or verb.

absolutely	nearly
actually	obviously
basically	particular
certain, certainly	plainly
clearly	practically
completely	pretty much
deepest	quite
extremely	really
frankly	so (as in "so great")
generally	sort of
given	surely
greatly	truly
in effect	various
kind of	very
more or less	virtually

1. The surface of the material *basically* was *very* rough and extremely discolored.

Revised: The surface of the material was rough and discolored.

2.   The tide was *obviously* faster than the owner's engineers had calculated, making the owner *clearly* liable for its *completely* inadequate construction plan.

Revised: The tide was faster than the owner's engineers had calculated, making the owner liable for the inadequacy of its construction plan.

Words that convey absolute qualities must remain unqualified if they are to retain their meaning, for example, "perfect," "dead," "absolute," "equal," "essential," "matchless," "mortal," "universal," "supreme," and "unique."

(i) Use Few Literary Devices

A plain style is usually the best style. If you do wish to use figurative language, do so where it will not interfere with communication of substance. When you edit or revise, consider the sensory dimension of words. Omit rhyme ("however clever"), cacophony ("egalitarian document"), conspicuous alliteration ("fallibility of four factfinders"), and unintentional puns ("a case without appeal").

Clichés come readily to mind during writing. Thus, a standard part of your revision should be to remove them or to renovate them. For example, you might play on the common cliché "adding insult to injury" by writing "adding insult to perjury," but remove such clichés as "height of absurdity," "day of reckoning," and "cold light of reason."

(j) Avoid Jargon From Other Fields

Words go in and out of fashion. Vague psychoanalytic terms, such as "interaction" and "supportive" were frequently used for a time before they gave way to computer jargon, such as "interface" and "input." Avoid word fads altogether. Words in fashion are quickly degraded; their specific meaning disappears, leaving only a vague colloquial meaning.

§ 5.3 A FEW BRIEF WORDS: REDUNDANCY IN LEGAL WRITING

As most lawyers know, redundant wording has a long and respectable past. Our Anglo–Saxon ancestors gave us word pairings, such as "safe and sound." After the Norman Invasion, French synonyms were added to the Middle English word pairs. Thus many legal terms have come to us in triplicate, for example, "give (Old English), devise (Old French) and bequeath (Old English)." Some word pairings are still commonly used, such as "acknowledge and confess," "act and deed," "deem and consider," "fit and proper,", "goods and chattels," "keep and maintain," "pardon and forgive," "shun and avoid," "aid and abet," "cease and desist," "fraud and deceit," and "null and void." Before automatically adopting an archaic word pairing, consider whether both words are needed.

Unnecessary word pairing continues to be a habit in modern English. If you think about each word you use, you will avoid redundancies such as the following.

basic fundamentals	telling revelation
basic starting point	terrible tragedy

false misrepresentation	true facts
final result	unexpected surprise
if and when	unless and until
sufficient enough	save and except

A more pervasive form of redundancy is the throw-away phrase, such as:

a certain amount of	as a matter of fact
due to the fact that	all intents and purposes
in case of	the nature of the case is
in regard to	the necessity of
the fact of the matter is	with reference to

Watch for these phrases when you edit and gradually train yourself to omit them during initial drafting.

Many other unnecessary words litter professional prose. As an editing technique, ask the question, "Do I need this word?" for each word in your next few writing projects. You will begin instinctively to pare away such unnecessary words and phrases as these:

Wordy	*Revised*
am hopeful that	hope
at that point in time	then
by means, reason, or virtue of	by
despite the fact that	although, even though
give recognition to	recognize
have knowledge of	know
in accordance with	by, under
in order to	to
in relation to	about
in the majority of instances	usually

is applicable to	applies to
is dependent on	depends on
make application to	apply to
make provision for	provide for
provides with an example of	exemplifies
until such time as	until

While redundancy wastes a reader's time, repetition of key words saves a reader's time. From sentence to sentence, key nouns and verbs should be repeated. The line between helpful repetition and redundancy is thin, but with experience the legal writer will develop a sense for where that line is.

§ 5.4 GLOSSARY OF WORDS COMMONLY MISUSED IN LEGAL WRITING

Every legal writer should regularly consult a standard usage text. This glossary is not intended as a substitute. Rather, it is intended as a law-oriented supplement to standard references such as those cited in the Selected References at the end of this *Nutshell*.

above, as in the *above* theory. Usage experts acknowledge this use of *above* with a noun to be permissible but prefer reversed order (theory *above*) by analogy to other indicators of place (*e.g., below*). Use of *above* with a verb is more precise (*e.g., above*-mentioned theory, theory summarized *above*) because what has been done *above* is identified. All of these usages are to be preferred to *aforesaid* in legal prose.

abstruse, obtuse. *Abstruse* is an adjective meaning "hard to understand." *Obtuse* is an adjective meaning "dull, insensitive in perception or imagination, slow to understand." A lawyer's reasoning may be *abstruse* because the lawyer is *obtuse*.

accuse, accused, as in *The plaintiffs were accused of conspiracy to defraud creditors.*

1.   The preposition *of* is correct.

2.   Use of *accuse* in relation to a civil fault is incorrect. In non-legal usage *accuse* means "to charge with a fault or an offense." In legal usage it has been limited to charging a crime.

adverse, averse. *Adverse* is an adjective meaning "against, opposed, harmful, or unfavorable," as in *adverse to the plaintiff's position*. *Averse* is an adjective meaning "unwilling, reluctant, or set against," with connotations of distaste or repugnance, as in *Law students are sometimes averse to rigorous writing exercises.*

affect, effect.

1.   As nouns. *Effect* is probably the word you want to use. It means "result or accomplishment." *Affect* (*af 'fect*—accent on the first syllable) is a psychological term that you will rarely have occasion to use in legal prose. (It refers to the conscious subjective aspect of an emotion.)

2.   As verbs. Confusion of the two words commonly occurs in their use as verbs. *Effect* means "to

bring about, to accomplish." *Affect* (accent on the last syllable) means "to influence."

allege, allegation.

1. *Allege* is spelled without a "d" before the "g."

2. *Allege* means "to declare or assert without proof." Do not use it when you mean contend or argue in the sense of giving reasons for or against something.

alternate, alternative.

1. *Alternate* as an adjective means "by turns." The derived adverb has the same meaning, as in *Defendant's two lawyers sought to question witnesses alternately*.

Alternative as an adjective means "offering a choice between two or more possibilities." The derived adverb has the same meaning: *Appellant's counsel argued alternative theories—that there was no contract and that if there was, it was breached by the defendant. Or, she argued that there was no contract and, alternatively, that if there was a contract, it was breached by the defendant.*

2. *Alternative* as a noun also means "a choice between two or more incompatible possibilities," as in *There is no* [not *no other*] *alternative* or in *The only alternative is settlement or trial* (that is, the only choice is the choice between settlement or trial). The noun also has a secondary meaning, that is, one of the several incompatible possibilities to be chosen, as in these sentences: *The settlement alter-*

native is unattractive. The only alternatives are set-
tlement and trial.

3.   Do not use the adjective *alternative* as a syn-
onym *for new, other*, or *revised*.

among, between. *Among* is precisely used to
express a relation of more than two persons: *among
the four parties. Between* ("by-twain") is precisely
used to express a relation of two persons: *between
the two parties*. Therefore, the common contractual
language *among and between parties A, B, and C* is
not a redundancy. It means: among A, B, and C;
between A and B, B and C, and A and C. From its
first use, however, *between* has extended to more
than two things in some situations and is the only
word for expressing the relation of a physical thing
to many surrounding things, as *in the property
between the three rivers.*

and/or. Avoid this confusing usage. *And/or* may
be interpreted as (i) both *and* and *or,* (ii) either *and*
or *or* but not both. In other expressions, the slash
stands for the words "or" or "per." Therefore,
and/or should carry the second meaning (ii). Because its usage is erratic, however, legal writers
should state what is intended: *fined or imprisoned
or both* rather than *fined and/or imprisoned.*

anticipate, expect. These words should not be
used synonymously. Use *expect* to mean "to look for
as likely to occur" or "to look for as necessary or
proper," as in *We expect the judge to grant a continuance*. Use *anticipate* to mean "to forestall, to take
steps beforehand, to use or enjoy in advance, to do

something before someone else," as in *Opposing counsel anticipated our strategy and moved for a continuance*.

appeal. To *appeal* (verb) means "to seek review of a decision in a legal action as a matter of right." If review is not available as of right, but only within a court's discretion, then one *applies for a writ* (*e.g.*, of certiorari).

appellee, appellant. See **parties in litigation**.

argue, contend, maintain. Courts do not *contend, maintain, or argue*. Counsel *contend* and *argue*. Courts *hold, decide, reason, state, suggest, imply, conclude*.

as. Do not use the conjunction *as* when you mean "since," "because," "when," or "while." Its broad and vague meanings can create confusion. For example, *As a potential work stoppage threatened to block the opening of school, the arbitrators revised the wording of the contract*. Does *as* mean "when," "because," or "while"?

as if, like. Do not use *like* in place of *as if*: *The judge proceeded as if* [not *like*] *counsel had raised no objection*.

as, like. *As*, as a conjunction, is used to introduce a clause (a verb must follow *as*): *Students must learn to think as lawyers do*. *Like*, as a preposition, is used for comparisons: *Students must learn to think like lawyers*.

as such, as in *The court limited the decision to subsequent cases; as such, the decision does not* *affect our case. Such* is here used as a pronoun. It should therefore have a referent. Its use seems most justified when a comparison is to be made, for example, *It was a prospective decision; as such it does not affect our case. As an indication of the court's attitude, however, it is significant.*

assume, assumption. *Assume* means "to accept as granted that something is true or accurate." Do not use the word or its derivatives when you mean "conclude," that is, to accept something on the basis of reasoning.

attorney, counsel, counselor, lawyer. The distinctions have been explained as follows: *Lawyer* is a general term, designating one who practices law. *Attorney* refers to one who has been designated to transact business for another (that is, a lawyer who has a client). A *counsel* is one who gives legal advice. *Counselor* means the same thing as *counsel*; it is most commonly used in court as a term of address. See also **counsel, counselor**.

based on, as in *Based on this decision, our client may be held liable for a breach of contract.* This use of *based on* is common but incorrect. In the example, *based on* modifies *our client*, thus suggesting that *our client was based on this decision*. To correct the example, substitute *given* for *based on*. (Note also the use of *breach* as a noun. Purists would object to the expression *for breaching the contract*, although dictionaries now bless the use of *breach* as a verb.)

basic, basically. Basic means "fundamental." The derived adverb, basically, should not be used as an introductory word without any clear meaning, as in these sentences: *Basically, I am reluctant to recommend that we go to trial. Basically, the statute is not clearly drafted.*

basis, as in *on the basis of*. Single prepositions or other more precise phrases can often be substituted for this jargon phrase, *e.g.*, substitute *under* in *It is nowhere stated that entitlement on the basis of section 416(h)(7)(A) must be full entitlement.* Substitute *by* in *Our client will be judged on the basis of the new standard.* Substitute *on* in *The case was presented to the court on the basis of certified questions.*

between. See **among, between**.

blatant. *Blatant* means "noisy, clamorous, obtrusive." It is often used when *flagrant* is intended as in this sentence: *This result is in blatant conflict with the purpose of the Act.* Even the correct use of *flagrant*, meaning "gross, openly evil," is usually overstatement or over-argument in legal prose.

breach, as a verb. See **based on**.

by, as in *by January 15*. The phrase is ambiguous. Does it mean *before* January 15 or *on or before* January 15? Say which you mean.

case.

1.   *Case* signifies, among other things, a dispute regularly and properly before a court for resolution. Do not personify *case,* as in *The Sutton case so held*. (Rather, write *In the Sutton case, the court so held*).

Do not write *This case presented itself to the court on certified questions*. (Rather, write *This case was presented to the court on certified questions*.)

2.   Do not use *where* with *case* when you mean *in which* or *wherein*: *The most significant case is United Labor, where the court so held*. Instead, use *in which the court so held*.

3.   Do not use *case* when you mean *court* or *opinion*. See **court 4**.

4.   *Case* may also refer to a dispute or other matter not yet before a court for resolution. Because the word can be used in the two different senses, it should be used with clear modifiers to avoid confusion. For example, if you use *this case* in a law office memorandum, it may not be clear whether you are referring to a decided *case* that you have just cited or to the client's *case* about which the memorandum is written. If you use *this case* in a brief, it might be taken as a reference to a decided *case* previously cited or to the *case* in which the argument is being presented. Here are some frequently used forms of reference that avoid such confusion. For decided cases: use an abbreviated part of the case title (for example, *Brinkly*) or use *that case* or *the cited case*. For your client's case: *The case before this court* or *our case*. *Case at hand* and *instant case* are also commonly used, but may seem pretentious.

5.   In a more general sense, *case* is used for a situation, a set of circumstances, an instance, an example, and other less clearly defined referents. It

has been imbedded in trite phrases that have, at best, no meaning, or at worst, an ambiguous meaning, *e.g., in the case of, in any case.* When tempted to use a phrase containing *case,* consider (a) whether the phrase is necessary and (b), if it is, whether a more precise word can be substituted for *case.*

citation, cite.

1.   In legal writing, indications of authorities are called *citations,* not *references.*

2.   *Cite* is a verb. It should not be used in place of *citation,* as in *The plaintiff's citations* [not *cites*] *are inaccurate.*

claim. This word has a special meaning under federal civil procedure rule 8(a), relating to *claims for relief.* More generally, it also means "to assert or demand a right or title to something." Unfortunately, it is commonly used incorrectly for *allege, state, declare, argue, argument, or conclude.* One student managed to squeeze most of these different meanings into one paragraph: *One claim[1] that could be made is that the Commission does not have the power to impose a sanction. Plaintiff could also claim[2] that the action cannot lie since the complaint does not claim[3] any arrest or seizure of property and special injury, which the Washington court has held is necessary in any claim[4] for malicious prosecution. Translations:* [1]*argument,* [2]*argue,* [3] *allege or aver and* [4]*claim*—correctly used in the special sense of civil procedure. Here is another misuse. *The court claimed that the minority position was erroneous.*

Claimed should be *concluded* or some other verb. See **argue, contend, maintain**.

compare to, compare with. We *compare* one case *with* another (examine similarities and differences) but *compare* a cliché *to* a comfortable old shoe (liken one thing to another).

compose, comprise. *Compose* means "to make up" or "to constitute." *Comprise* means "to be composed of" or "to consist of." *The American Digest System comprises nine units and a current supplement* (or *is composed of*). *Nine units and a current supplement compose the American Digest System* (or *are comprised in*).

conclusions of law. See **find, finding**.

conform. A contract may *conform* to law or be *in conformity with law*. Goods may *conform to* description or be *in conformity with* description.

construction, interpretation. These words are commonly used interchangeably to refer to the process of determining the meaning of contracts and statutes. A useful distinction has been suggested, however, in *3 Corbin on Contracts 9* (1960): "[T]he word *interpretation* is commonly used with respect to language itself—to the symbols (the words and acts of expression ... By 'interpretation of the language' we determine what ideas that language induces in other persons). By 'construction of the contract' ... we determine it legal operation—its effect upon the action of courts and administrative officials."

contain. Search for a more precise verb if you are tempted to say something like this: *The Rosenberg opinion contains several relevant factors that should be developed in our case. (identifies? suggests? summarizes?)*

contend. See **argue, contend, maintain**.

continual, continuous. *Continual* means "frequently or closely repeated." *Continuous* means "without interruption."

contract. One is a party *to*, not *of*, a contract. But, does one *enter* or *enter into* a contract? The latter seems to be the correct usage (though the former occasionally appears in otherwise carefully written court opinions): one *enters* a transaction on the books but *enters into* an association.

counsel, counselor. Note the correct spelling for the words used to describe one who gives legal advice. Note also that *counsel* is the correct form for both singular and plural. See also **attorney, counsel, counselor, lawyer.**

court.

1.   A court with more than one judge is an entity (*it*), not a collection of individuals (*they*). If the judges are not unanimous in deciding a case, then you may refer to *the majority of the court* and the *dissenting* (or *concurring*) *judges* or to *dissenters*. See **dissent**. You may also refer to the majority's decision as the decision of *the court* (or *the Court* if you are referring to the United States Supreme Court). If you are reporting a particular judge's

view (for example, that of a concurring or dissenting judge), use *Judge* _____; for the United States Supreme Court and some state supreme courts, use *Justice* _____. (Note that *Mr. Justice* _____ is no longer used for United States Supreme Court justices. The "Mr." has been dropped in accordance with notice by Associate Justice Stevens to the clerk's office. *National Law Journal*, Dec. 1, 1980, at 55, col. 1, 2.)

2.   Either *judge* or *court* may be used to refer to a court with a single judge, for example, for a trial court.

3.   Do not substitute the name of a jurisdiction for *court*. For example, *California has held* is incorrect; it should be *the California court has held* if reference is to the highest court in the state, or *a California court has held* if the reference is to other than the highest court.

4.   Do not substitute *case* or *opinion* for *court* or *judge*. For example, *the Graham case so held* is incorrect; it should be *In the Graham case, the California court so held*.

criteria. *Criteria* is a plural noun. The singular is *criterion*.

deals with, as in *The federal regulation specifically deals with "cooperation" in obtaining support*. This phrase is often a fuzzy substitute for a more descriptive verb. Here, for example, the writer may have meant that the regulation *defines "cooperation,"* or *specifies when "cooperation" may be re-*

quired. The more precise explanation should be provided.

decide, decision. See **hold, holding**.

deed, quitclaim deed, title.

1.   It is the *deed*, not the title that is *delivered and recorded*.

2.   *Quitclaim* is correct, not *quick*claim. *Quitclaim* is not hyphenated.

defendant. See **parties in litigation**.

dicta, dictum.

1.   *Dicta* is plural; a *dictum* is singular.

2.   *Dicta* are statements in a court opinion that are not necessary to the court's resolution of the problem before it, or, stated in another way, they are answers to questions not presented. Thus, the words *dicta* and *holdings* are mutually exclusive. Therefore, it is gross error to say that a court *held in dicta*; rather a court *states in dicta*. If the correct characterization is in doubt, use an expression like *stated in what may be dicta* and explain the reason for doubt. *Binding dicta* is equally objectionable.

different.

1.   Use *different from* rather than *different than* and you will usually be safe. Thus, a case may be *different from* a previously decided case.

2.   Do not use "no" with *different from* as in this sentence: *The conclusion reached by the scholars is that the rule in defamation cases should be no different from the rule in other cases*. (Rather, *the*

rule in defamation cases should not be different from or should not differ from.)

disinterested, uninterested. *Disinterested* means "free from bias and self-interest." *Uninterested* means "not interested or apathetic." The distinction must be observed in legal contexts. In an administrative proceeding, the hearing official must be *disinterested*; whether he or she is *uninterested* is usually not legally significant.

dissent. Do not use *dissent* as a substitute for *dissenters, dissenting judges*, or *dissenting opinion*. Examples: *The dissent based on its conclusion on a fiction rather than on public policy.* (Rather, *The dissenters* [or *dissenting judges*] *based their conclusion on a fiction rather than on public policy.*) *The reasons for the differing views were detailed in the dissent.* (Rather, *The reasons for the differing views were detailed in the dissenting opinion.*) See also **court** 1.

doubtless, no doubt, undoubtedly. *Doubtless,* as an adverb, and *no doubt* have lost the literal sense of "without doubt." Now they merely suggest probability or concession, as in *The court doubtless considered the possibility* and *No doubt other opinions exist.* To express the absence of doubt, use *undoubtedly, without a doubt,* or *beyond a doubt.*

due to.

1. *Caused by, resulting from,* or *because of* will be more precise expressions than *due to* in such sentences as these: *The court allowed the tenant to recover for personal injuries due to the landlord's*

negligent maintenance. (Rather, for personal injuries resulting from the landlord's negligent maintenance.) This reasoning will become more appealing in light of the injustice suffered by litigants due to extensive court delays. (Rather, in light of injustice suffered by litigants because of extensive court delays.)

2. *Due to* is often superfluous in the statement of a reason, as in this sentence: *The reason for distinguishing the cases may be due to different characteristics of the two types of vehicles.* (Rather, *The reason for distinguishing the cases may be the different characteristics of the two types of vehicles.*)

easy, easily, readily. These are often whistling-in-the-dark words, as in *It is easy to argue that* or *It could readily be argued that*, Avoid such usages. State what you mean: That a point could be *persuasively* or *authoritatively* so argued? That opposing counsel may be expected to so argue? That a careless attorney might so argue?

effect. See **affect**.

establishment. This word is often either incorrectly used or used in an awkward way (even though used correctly to mean "an act of establishing" or "state of being established"). Examples: *The establishment of the disclosure violation may be difficult.* (Rather, *Establishing the disclosure violation may be difficult.*) *Plaintiff's claim for benefits was barred by Mary Lou's establishment of her claim as Joseph's legal widow.* (Rather, *The claim was barred by Mary Lou's having previously estab-*

lished her claim.) The Secretary is charged with establishment of standards for state programs. (Rather, *The Secretary is charged with drafting or adopting standards.) The survey revealed that many deserting fathers could afford to make child support payments but do not—either through lack of establishment of lack of enforcement of obligations.* (Rather, *either because their duty is not established or is not enforced.*)

expect. See **anticipate, expect**.

explicit, implicit. Use these words in their literal, not their colloquial sense. *Implicit* means "implied, understood though unexpressed." Do not use it to mean "absolute, full, or complete," as in *implicit obedience*. The antithesis of *implicit* is *explicit*. Do not use it to mean "absolute, full or complete," as in *the one explicit payment* or in *that explicit group of people*. The opposites, *implied* and *expressed*, have not acquired colloquial meanings and so may be the wiser choices for the legal writer.

fact.

1.   The line between *fact* and *rule* may be indistinct, but it should not be ignored, as in this sentence: *This result is a reaction to the fact that the patent-child relationship alone is not sufficient to impute liability*. The writer was clearly noting the effect of a *rule*, not a *fact*.

2.   *The true facts are stated in the record*. Strike *true*. *Facts* are true by definition. But a *statement of facts* may be untrue or inaccurate.

3. See **find, finding**.

farther, further. Distinctions between these two words seem to be disappearing. You will not be faulted, however, if you confine your use of *farther* to describe physical distance. Thus, *The court reasoned further that* ...

feel, as in *The court felt that the result was justified* or in *I feel* ...

1. A *court* does not *feel*, and we ordinarily cannot know how the *judges feel* about a case. Search for a more precise verb.

2.   Search for a more precise word also if you are tempted to say, "I feel ..." Usually you will realize that you *conclude, believe, assume, or infer*. Use *feel* only if you are making an intuitive or emotional statement.

few, fewer, less.

1.   *Fewer* means "a smaller number," as in *fewer people* (not *less people*) and *fewer mistakes, fewer words*. *Less* as a comparative means "a smaller amount of," as in *less pay*.

2.   Use *comparatively few*, not *a comparative few* or *the comparative few* (neither of which makes sense).

find, finding. Courts may *find facts*. *Findings of fact* are a court's determinations of the facts. The *findings* may be included in a document stating those factual determinations and also stating legal conclusions. The title of the document is "Findings of Fact and Conclusions of Law." The document, signed by the judge, is commonly required in cases tried before a judge without a jury.

guilty, liable. *Guilty* carries stronger implications of blameworthiness than *liable*. It implies consciousness of crime or moral wrong. Hence, it is appropriate to say that a person is *guilty of a crime* but *liable for negligence* (or other civil fault).

heavily, as in *The court relied heavily on distinguishable precedents*. The word is trite and imprecise. Did the court rely *exclusively*? *primarily*? *in part*?

hold, holding, decide, decision

1. *Holding* refers to the result reached by a court in resolving a case regularly and properly before it. That result may also be called a *decision* (though *decision* may also be used in a more general sense). A *holding* is unique because it can refer only to the result on the facts and for the parties in a particular case. Neither *holding* nor *decision* should be used to refer to a *rule*, which is a more general statement that explains many cases. (But see **rule, ruling** 3.) Example: *The court applied the rule that a violation of a zoning ordinance is not an encumbrance that renders title unmarketable. It then held that the violation of the Seattle ordinance that restricted use of the building on the defendant's property did not render the defendant's title unmarketable. Holding* may also refer to the result in a case in a procedural sense, as in *The court's holding that the complaint should be dismissed was in error.*

These observations apply also to the verbs *hold* and *decide*.

2.   Courts *hold*. Rules do not. Therefore use of *holds* in the following sentence is both wrong and redundant: *Our client's position will be affected by the rule that holds that evidence of remarriage must not be admitted.*

3.   Since *hold* and *holding* have a technical meaning, their use in general or non-technical senses should be avoided, as in *This argument does not hold* or in *The court holds [reasons] that such information would mislead the jury.*

idea. This word is used vaguely to express a number of "ideas" that should be more precisely identified, as in these sentences: *In McDonald the court directly addressed the assumption of risk idea.* (Assumption of risk *defense?*) *The Washington court deals unfavorably with the idea concerning public policy.* (Public policy *argument?*) *Analysis of the idea suggests that the Washington court would allow disclosure.* (Analysis of the *rationale?* the *criticism?*)

impact. As a noun *impact* means "the forceful striking of one thing against another, a collision." Do not use it figuratively to mean "effect or influence" as in this sentence: *The impact of the court's decision cannot be predicted as this time.*

implicit. See **explicit, implicit.**

imply, infer. *Imply* means "to suggest or to say indirectly." *Infer* means "to surmise or to draw a conclusion from something written or spoken by someone else." Thus, a court may *imply* a conclusion in its opinion, but a reader will *infer* the conclusion from the court's opinion.

in terms of. This phrase is commonly used as a substitute for a precise identification of relationship or as a substitute for such prepositions as *at, by, as*, or *for*. The phrase is correctly used when one thing is being expressed *in terms of* another thing, as when a rule is discussed *in terms of* its economic effect. The phrase is loosely or incorrectly used in the following sentences: *This policy argument is strong in terms of our client's case.* (Is a strong argument for our client? Or for the opposition?) *If the doctor's words are construed in terms of a guarantee, the result will be different.* (Construed *as* a guarantee?)

interpretation. See **construction**.

issue.

1. An *issue* is a question that can be answered in more than one way, a point of dispute or controversy. *Issue* should not be used vaguely or unnecessarily. For example, in *The issue of assignment is not disputed*, the word is used improperly. What is not disputed? The *existence* of an assignment? The *validity* of an assignment? In the following sentence, the introductory phrase is used unnecessarily: *The issue of whether the assignment was valid was decided without reference to the controlling precedent.* If the *issue* has been previously stated, the sentence may be correctly written without "*The*

issue of" or even more concisely, *The assignment issue was decided without reference to the controlling precedent.*

2. The following phrases should be distinguished: *In issue* refers to points that are in controversy or disputed, particularly those issues that are properly before a court. *At issue* refers to issues that are ready for decision, ready to go to the trier of fact (judge or jury).

it is, there is. Sentences beginning with these words can often be rewritten more concisely and more directly. For example, *It is uncertain as to which procedure the agency must follow* can be more directly written as *Which procedure the agency must follow is uncertain.* The sentence *There is no provision in the statute for rescission if the notice is given* can be more concisely written as *The statute does not provide for rescission if the notice is given.*

judge, justice. See **court** 1.

judgment. When used to mean the terminal decision or document in litigation, *judgment* is spelled without the middle "e" in American legal materials, although use of that "e" ("judgement") is an accepted variant spelling in English legal materials and in other settings.

jurisdiction. This word is commonly used in two senses: to refer to a court system (for example, the federal *jurisdiction*) and to refer to the power of a court or a court system to hear and decide particular disputes. Do not use *jurisdiction* in the former sense when you are actually referring to a particular court. See **court** 3.

lawyer. See **attorney, counsel, counselor, lawyer**.

less. See **few, fewer, less**.

liable, liability.

1.   See **guilty**.

2.   *Liability* is *imposed on* a party to litigation, *not fastened on, placed on,* or *procured.*

like. See **as, like** and **as if, like**.

likely.

1.   When *likely* is used as an adverb, it ought to be modified by a qualifying word like *quite, very,* or *most* as in *A decision will most likely be given within ten days.*

2.   The colloquial misuse of *likely* instead of *probably* in the following examples is becoming too common: *There will likely be a change* and *Its validity as a contract will likely be challenged.*

ludicrous, as in *It is ludicrous to say that Congress intended this result in such a small class of cases.* This word means "inept, foolish, or exaggerated to the point of absurdity." To so characterize an opposing counsel's argument or a court's rationale is to over argue or overstate.

maintain. See **argue**.

memoranda, memorandum. The singular form is *memorandum.*

no doubt. See **doubtless, no doubt, undoubtedly**.

obtuse. See **abstruse, obtuse**.

opinion. A court *opinion* is the official written statement of a court's decision in a case and its reasons for reaching the decision. For appropriate usage, see **court** 4.

oral, verbal. *Oral* means "spoken or uttered." *Verbal* means "with words or consisting of words, either written or spoken." Thus, *whether in writing or verbal* makes no sense; it should be *whether written or oral*.

overrule, reverse.

1.   A court *overrules* its prior decisions and the decisions of lower courts within its jurisdiction. A court reverses a lower court judgment in the specific case before it, for example, *After holding that the precedent on which the lower court relied should be overruled, the supreme court held that the judgment for plaintiff should be reversed*. See also **rule, ruling** 3.

2.   A decision is *overruled* only when the subsequent decision is directly contrary to the earlier decision. If the later decision is not directly contrary, then the earlier decision may be *limited* or *modified*.

3.   Dicta are *disapproved*, not *overruled*.

4.   Courts also *overrule* objections.

5. *Overrule* is sometimes used with respect to motions (applications to courts for orders), but *deny* seems to be the correct verb.

parol, parole. *Parol* is a noun or adjective meaning *oral*, as in *parol evidence* or *parol lease* or *proof by parol*. *Parole* is a noun or a verb meaning *conditional release of a prisoner*.

parties in litigation.

1. A suit may be commenced by a *plaintiff* or by a *petitioner*, the latter term being used in some equity proceedings and in applications for extraordinary writs, such as mandamus or quo warranto. The party sued is a *defendant* (spelled with an "ant," not an "ent").

2. One who appeals as a matter of right will usually be called the *appellant*. The other party may be a *respondent* (spelled with an "ent," not an "ant") or an *appellee*. The choice apparently depends on which term happens to be used in the controlling rules or statutes. One who seeks review that is discretionary with a court (see **appeal**) is a *petitioner*.

3. In text, capitalize the title of a party (*e.g.*, plaintiff, appellant) only if you are using it as a formal title or as a substitute for a proper name, omitting "the," for example: Plaintiff telephoned Defendant [or Defendant Jones] several times but failed to reach her. But: The plaintiff telephoned the defendant several times.

petitioner, plaintiff. See **parties in litigation**.

precedence, precedents. *Precedents* are court decisions that may be followed by courts in subsequent cases presenting the same legal problem. Precedence means "priority, the fact of preceding in time."

principal, principle. Remember the different spellings for three different meanings: The principal [primary] objection to the liability principle [general and fundamental rule] is that the agent's principal [one who employs another to act] escapes all liability.

question of. This phrase is often used to introduce something that is not a question or that should be stated as a "whether" clause. For example, *The question of protective payments depends on two determinations*. Either a more precise word should be selected (*the propriety of protective payments* or *the need for protective payments*) or the question should be stated, for example: *Whether protective payments should be made depends on two determinations*. Or, if the question has been previously stated, then, *The answer to the protective payment question depends on two determinations*.

quitclaim deed. See **deed**.

quote. Do not use this verb for the noun *quotation*. For example, *Both attorneys and law students tend to use too may quotes* [should be *quotations*] *in their briefs*.

re. *Re* means *in the matter of*. It is correctly used in the case title for certain kinds of legal proceedings (*In re* Jones) or in a non-textual introductory statement for a letter to identify the subject matter (preceding the text of the letter, thus: *Re: Jones v. Allen*). In text, use *regarding, about*, or *concerning*, for example, *I am writing to you about the appeal in the Jones case.*

respective, respectively. Do not use these words unnecessarily as in *The lawyers presented their respective theories in extended oral arguments*. Rather, use them when necessary to clarify the relationships between sets of things and sets of their modifiers: *Under the will, Peter, Francy, and Kenneth respectively are to receive the antique shop, the farm, and the residue.* (This sentence is simpler than the alternative: *Under the will, Peter is to receive the antique shop, Francy is to receive the farm, and Kenneth is to receive the residue.*)

response, as in **in response to**. This phrase is often used incorrectly without a verb, as in the following sentences: *The regulations were [adopted] in response to the problem created by lack of definitions. Board Letter No. 829 was [written] in response to an inquiry about disclosure of a security interest in all after-acquired property.*

rule, ruling.

1. See **hold, holding**.

2. Give thought to selection of a precise verb in describing what a court does with reference to a rule. For example, rules may be *reaffirmed* (if previously applied by the same court), *adopted, accepted*, or *stated*. Use of *laid down, set down*, or *set forth* normally reflects inexperience in legal writing.

3. **The court reversed the rule** is incorrect. *Judgments*, not *rules*, get reversed. (*Rules* are *no longer followed*.) A court's *ruling*, on the other hand, may be *reversed*. A *ruling* is a court's determination or order made during litigation, as in deciding pre-trial motions or points during trial. For example, a court may apply the hearsay *rule* in *ruling* that the evidence would not be admitted.

tenant, tenet. Do not confuse the spellings. A *tenant* occupies rented premises. A *tenet* is a doctrine regarded as true, particularly by a group.

there is. See **it is**.

this. This word accounts for much fuzzy legal writing. It is used to refer indefinitely to entire paragraphs of a preceding discussion. It is used to refer to ideas, arguments, reasoning, or things not previously mentioned. Avoid such indefinite references by following the simple rule never to use "this" without adding a word that identifies what "this" refers to. For example, *This [rule] opens the way for indiscriminate seizure. This [conclusion] is further substantiated in a case decided last year. This [lack of distinction] is what leads me to conclude that the Harold decision will be controlling. In 1960 the statute was amended; this [amendment] was intended to broaden the statute to cover new types of contracts. (Better: In 1960 the statute was amended to extend its coverage to new types of contracts.)*

title. See **deed**.

undoubtedly. See **doubtless, no doubt, undoubtedly**.

unique. *Unique* is an adjective meaning one of a kind. Do not use it to mean *unusual* or *remarkable*. A case is either *unique* or it is *not unique*: it cannot be *somewhat unique* or *most unique*.

verbal. See **oral, verbal**.

CHAPTER 6

PUNCTUATION AND GRAMMAR

§ 6.1 INTRODUCTION

Legal writers must have full command of punctuation and grammar. Punctuation tells the reader how to read a sentence or paragraph. Thus, the legal writer must punctuate precisely in order to control meaning. This "tight" punctuation requires a better understanding of the basic rules than many undergraduates have before they enter law school. "Loose" punctuation, punctuation that yields more than one interpretation, is permitted and sometimes encouraged in undergraduate writing courses. The legal writer, however, should never punctuate loosely. Doing so creates the risk of misreading by a judge, another lawyer, or a client.

The punctuation section in this chapter covers those rules most commonly violated by law students and lawyers. The rules receiving greatest emphasis are those that prevent ambiguity and that save the reader from having to reread for comprehension.

Grammar refers to syntax, that is, to sentence structure. As young children we learn to speak grammatically. If we did not, no one would understand us. An ungrammatical "sentence" might be: "Documented doubtful the was fully claim." As

English speakers, we know how to make that grammatical. Without much effort, we can arrange it meaningfully in several ways, all determined by the grammar of our language: "The doubtful claim was fully documented." "Fully documented was the doubtful claim." "The doubtful claim was documented fully." Grammar also refers to the "operating principles" of our language, for example, correct use of inflections and parts of speech. It is ungrammatical to say "The letter was signed by him and I" (rather than me). For most native speakers, grammar is instinctive and understandable. However, if a child learns to speak ungrammatically in a particular way, and if that child's schooling does not correct the error, then as an adult speaker and writer, he or she may have an ungrammatical habit. The section below on grammar is intended to point out the most common of these ungrammatical habits.

§ 6.2 PUNCTUATION

(a) Introduction

In legal writing, there are no significant variations from standard usage. While writing, use a standard grammar or usage handbook as a desk reference. If you are unable to find a solution to a punctuation problem in this Nutshell or in your handbook, at least punctuate consistently in the same piece of writing.

(b) Use of the Comma

(1) *Use a Compound Sentence Comma for Clarity*

Use a comma to separate two independent clauses joined by "and," "but," "or," "for," "nor," or "yet." The comma precedes the conjunction.

Confusing: The plaintiff's car hit the road block and the defendant failed to stop. (The reader may at first think that the car hit the road block and the defendant. The appearance of "failed" sends the reader back to re-read the sentence.)

Clear: The plaintiff's car hit the road block, and the defendant failed to stop. (The comma signals a completed unit of thought. The reader is then prepared for a new subject in a new clause.)

(2) *Do Not Use a Comma With Compound Subjects, Verbs, and Objects*

Legal writers use interior coordination frequently; that is, they use compound subjects, verbs, and objects, joined by coordinating conjunctions. These are often mispunctuated, as in the following examples.

1. *Incorrect division of a compound verb*: The Trust Fund suspended payments to plaintiff effective in April, and further determined that contributions received on his behalf should be refunded.

Corrected: The Trust fund suspended payments to plaintiff effective in April and further determined that contributions received on his behalf should be refunded.

2. *Incorrect division of a compound object*: The appellants contend that the facts alleged by appellants were not sufficient to constitute duress, and that the

case was controlled by *Ingebrigt v. Seattle Taxicab and Transfer Co.*

Corrected: The appellants contend that the facts alleged by appellants were not sufficient to constitute duress and that the case was controlled by *Ingebrigt v. Seattle Taxicab and Transfer Co.*

(3) Use Two Commas to Set Off Interruptions

Commas are used to enclose parenthetical, explanatory, or interruptive words, phrases, or clauses. These commas mark the boundaries of a phrase or clause. Thus, use two unless one is replaced by a period or other mark of punctuation.

1. A lawyer, with a stroke of the pen, can save an estate from bankruptcy.

2. The plaintiff's car hit the utility pole, according to witnesses, and thus caused a three-hour power outage.

3. Will you help us sort through the files, at your convenience, to find the missing deposition?

(4) Use Commas for Nonrestrictive Phrases or Clauses

One essential use of the interrupting comma is to indicate nonrestriction, that is, a commenting word, phrase, or clause. Conversely, the absence of an interrupting comma indicates restriction, that is, a limiting word, phrase, or clause. For example, the interrupting commas in the following example tell us that there is only one defendant, not several: "The defendant, the Minamoto Corporation, requests dismissal of the charge." If there were more than one defendant, the commas would be omitted:

"Defendant Minamoto Corporation requests dismissal of the charge."

A simple way to illustrate the difference between restriction and nonrestriction is by limiting or not limiting a category:

Category: tort

Restriction: a tort that involves a breach of contract

Nonrestriction (explanatory, not limiting); a tort, which ordinarily falls within the civil domain

(5) Use a Comma With "Which" But Not With "That"

The use of "that" signals a limiting function; in other words, it introduces a restriction of the preceding word or phrase.

Restrictive: The judges will read the briefs that are well written. (Only the well-written briefs will be read.)

The use of "which" signals a non-defining function; in other words, it does not restrict the preceding word or phrase.

Nonrestrictive: The judges will read the briefs, which are well written. (All the briefs will be read, and all the briefs are well written.)

Since many writers use "which" for both defining and non-defining clauses, a comma must be used to make the distinction clear. A comma preceding a "which" clause signals a non-defining function. Absence of a comma signals that the clause is defining.

(6) Do Not Use a Comma to Separate a Long or Compound Subject From Its Verb

If the subject is so long that it needs a marker or boundary at the end, do not use the careless device of an incorrect comma. Rewrite or rephrase the sentence. This fault is commonly found in poorer legal prose.

Confusing: The dicta in recent Supreme Court opinions and the explicit recognition of that Court's authority by the lower courts, emphasize what was first developed in *Brown v. Waters*.

Clear: (Omit the comma and rewrite) The dicta in recent Supreme Court opinions emphasizes what was first developed in *Brown v. Waters*. The lower courts' explicit recognition of the Court's authority has furthered that development.

(7) Use an Introductory Comma to Set Off Introductory Words, Phrases, or Clauses

If the introductory element is short and no misreading is possible, the comma may be omitted, for example, "In 1975 the Corporation signed a collective bargaining agreement."

Examples that invite misreading:

1. *Confusing omission of comma*: To summarize the question is difficult.

Clear. To summarize, the question is difficult. Or: The question is difficult to summarize.

2. *Confusing*: Contrary to the holding in *Bracton v. Blackstone* at that time the practice of submitting documentary evidence to a jury was long established.

Clear: Contrary to the holding in *Bracton v. Blackstone*, at that time the practice of submitting documentary evidence to a jury was long established.

(8) Use a Series Comma

Use a comma to mark each separate element in a series; that is, put a comma after each item and before the conjunction. (A, B, and C)

Confusing Omissions of Series Comma:

1.   Both jobs require activities that are closely related, such as the teaching of sports skills, the supervision and coordination of practices and competitive activities. (Comma belongs after "practices.")

2.   Although blood alcohol levels depend on various factors, including body weight, amount and type of food in the stomach and time between drinking and testing, the primary factor is the amount of alcohol ingested. (If no comma follows "stomach," the reader does not know where the series ends.)

3.   The witnesses included one representative from Washington, Oregon, Montana and Nevada and Utah. (One from Montana and Nevada and another from Utah? Or one from Montana and another from Nevada and Utah?)

(9) Use a Contrasting Comma for Emphasis

Use a comma to emphasize contrast or to add emphasis to a particular word, phrase, or clause.

He sold non-existent property in Washington, not in Oregon.

(10) Use a Comma to Separate Dependent from Independent Clauses

If the dependent clause comes first, it should be separated from the independent clause by a comma.

If the independent clause comes first, no comma is used if the dependent clause restricts the meaning of the independent clause.

1.   If an employee objects to a medical examination, the case must be considered individually.

2.   A case must be considered individually if an employee objects to a medical examination.

(11) Do Not Use a Comma Before "Because"

Do not use a comma before "because" unless "because" introduces a nonrestrictive clause. That rarely happens.

Incorrect: This is contradictory to the common practice, because, according to that practice, the title of ownership will not be transferred to the buyer until payment is completed.

Corrected: This is contradictory to the common practice because, according to that practice, the title of ownership will not be transferred to the buyer until payment is completed.

(12) Use a Comma to Separate Some Adjectives

Coordinate adjectives are those that may be joined by "and": erratic, vague testimony ("erratic" and "vague" both modify "testimony").

Use no comma if the first adjective modifies the second adjective, that is, if "and" is not understood between them (thus, they are not coordinate):

"a good looking man"

"illegal drug traffic"

"grey striped cat" (if the stripes are grey, but "grey, striped cat" if the cat is grey and striped)

(13) Use a Comma After Parenthetical Material

Use the comma after the parenthesis, not before.

Because the case was too old (1875), we omitted it.

(14) Place a Comma Inside Quotation Marks

Both a comma and a period are always placed inside quotation marks.

He is not classified as an "employee."

He is not an "employee," nor is he a union member.

(15) Use Commas With Numbers

Use a comma with dates, addresses, place names, statistics, measurements, and the like to increase readability.

January 18, 1980, (month and day, year,)

On January 18, 1,000 entries were received.

On 18 January 1980, we received your letter.

(c) Use of the Semicolon

(1) Use a Semicolon to Separate Two Sentences

Use a semicolon to separate two sentences:

(i) if joined without a connective:

It was 8:00 P.M.; the road was dry.

(ii) if joined with a conjunctive adverb, such as "however," "therefore," "moreover":

It was 8:00 P.M.; furthermore, the road was dry.

(iii) if joined with other transitional expressions, such as "in brief," "on the other hand":

It was 8: P.M.; contrary to testimony, the road was dry.

Do not use a semicolon if one sentence is incomplete (*i.e.*, a fragment), as in these examples:

1. Because lawyers are expected to think and speak well, they are expected to write well; when in fact many of them don't. (Use a comma instead of a semicolon since what follows the semicolon is a fragment.)

2. Mr. Gould replied that the NLRB would not discuss it; and would not need to. (The semicolon separates a compound verb and must be deleted.)

(2) Use a Semicolon to Substitute for the Comma in a Complex Series

A semicolon should be substituted for a comma when internal punctuation obscures the main divisions of any series:

The beneficiaries we must locate are Robert E. Kelley of Arcata, California; Shannon G. Squires of Samish Island, Washington; Helen Driver, who has recently moved to El Paso, Texas; W. F. Irmscher of Seattle, Washington; and Eleanor Laney of Dallas, Texas.

(3) Place a Semicolon Outside Quotation Marks

The witness replied, "I don't know"; however, the record shows that she did know.

When a direct quotation ends in a semicolon or colon, the semicolon or colon may be dropped.

(d) Use of the Colon

(1) Use a Colon to Introduce a List or an Enumeration

A colon may be used instead of a comma:

The plaintiff's legal position depends upon extracts from three decisions of the United States Supreme Court: *Anderson v. Shipowners, United Mine Workers v. Pennington*, and *Federal Maritime Commission v. Pacific Maritime Association*.

(2) Use a Colon to Indicate That Something Will Follow

What follows will usually be an example, illustration, or elaboration:

In *Anderson v. Shipowners*, the collective bargaining process was not used: a unilateral hiring procedure had already been set up by the Association.

(3) Use a Colon to Introduce Quotations or Formal Statements

The Court found that the activity was not permissible: "The shipowners have surrendered completely to the control of the Association, thus limiting the activities of both shipowners and seamen."

(4) Use a Colon to Emphasize What Follows

Not only is the report itself hearsay, but most of it is second-and third-level hearsay: the statements of numerous persons are summarized, quoted, or otherwise relied upon.

When a complete sentence follows a colon, the capital letter at the beginning of the sentence is optional.

Examples, both correct:

1. Lay readers can be helpful in several ways: (1) they have not been "desensitized" to the obfuscation and convolutions of legal writing, and (2) they can identify the words, sentences, or ideas that will be difficult for non-lawyers to understand.

2. Lay readers can be helpful in several ways: (1) They have not been "desensitized" to the obfuscation and convolutions of legal writing. (2) They can point out words, sentences, or ideas that will be difficult for non-lawyers to understand.

(5) Place a Colon Outside Quotation Marks

No one has denied Plaintiff's statement that "mortgage instruments should be comprehensible": the court agrees, the defendant agrees, and the general public agrees.

(e) Use of Parentheses

(1) Use Parentheses to Set Off Potentially Ambiguous Phrases

Sometimes parentheses are more reliable than commas for setting off phrases that are potentially ambiguous or that obscure the "main line" of the sentence.

Confusing: Borrowers must be informed of limits on transfer or sale of their property other than with the Bank's consent before they are asked to sign a loan instrument. (Does the bank consent before they sign?)

Clear: Borrowers must be informed of limits on transfer or sale of their property (other than with the Bank's consent) before they are asked to sign a loan instrument.

(2) Use Parentheses to Enclose Interruptions

Explanations, digressions, and other interruptions to the main thought of the sentence may be set off with parentheses.

The answer is "yes" and "no" (a lawyer-like response).

(3) Use Correct Punctuation With Parentheses

If the parentheses occur at the end of a sentence, the end punctuation goes outside the last parenthesis. If the parentheses contain a full sentence, punctuation goes inside the last parenthesis.

Law students must have writing exercises (as opposed to "search and destroy" missions in the library).

Law students must have writing exercises. (They should do more than "search and destroy missions" in the library.)

(4) Use Parentheses to Enclose Numbers and Letters Marking Divisions in the Main Text

A deed of trust must: (1) be comprehensible to lay readers, (2) accurately reflect the requirements of the lender, and (3) clearly inform lay borrowers of their obligations.

(f) Use of the Hyphen

Use a hyphen with a compound adjective when necessary to prevent ambiguity, as in "first-class," "well-written," "well-timed," "year-long," "decision-making," "job-related." As shown in the examples below, the problem is that one word may be read as the wrong part of speech.

1.   *Confusing*: The government financed research in the maritime industry is declining. (Is the research government-financed, or does the government finance research?)

With hyphen: The government-financed research in the maritime industry is declining.

2.   *Confusing:* Furthermore, the state sponsored schools throughout this area provide the greatest portion of NCAA funds. (Are the schools state-sponsored or does the state sponsor schools?)

With hyphen: Furthermore, the state-sponsored schools throughout this area provide the greatest portions of NCAA funds.

3.   *Confusing*: Watch for heavy vehicle traffic. (Heavy vehicles or heavy traffic?)

With hyphen: Watch for heavy-vehicle traffic. (Watch for heavy vehicles.)

Use a hyphen to form compounds with numbers:

Two-week trial

Thirty-five-year-old defendant

Five-year contract

(g) Use of a Dash

(1) Use the Dash Sparingly

The dash is the least defined mark of punctuation. It suggests a connection rather than describing it. The dash has connotations of stream-of-consciousness thought and carries a conversational tone.

The dash should be used sparingly in legal writing and then mainly to introduce a recapitulation. It may also be used strategically in an argument—for dramatic effect.

(2) Use a Dash to Indicate a Break, Shift, or Interruption

When law graduates begin to practice law—which for most lawyers means writing every day under pressure—they should already know how to write well.

(3) Use a Dash to Expand an Idea

Use of a dash to expand an idea is rhetorically effective when combined with repetition of a word or phrase.

As a result of this accident, the plaintiff sustained severe and lasting injuries—so severe that his foot may require amputation.

Leave no space before, after, or between the two hyphens that make up a dash.

(h) Use of the slash or Virgule

The slash has become increasingly popular in legal writing and is often misused. It should not be used to mean "and." It means "or." It indicates an "either-or" situation, that is, a choice of alternatives.

Do not use the slash for "and/or" if you mean both "and" and "or." It means one or the other, but not both. Do not use the slash for phrases like "public/private functions" if you mean both "public" and "private." It means "public" or "private," but not both.

Use a slash to indicate alternatives:

The car is available with a white/brown exterior and a black/beige interior.

The "will/shall" controversy is passé.

Use a slash to stand for "per" in abbreviation (40 mi./hr.).

(i) Use of Quotation Marks

Close quotation marks after a period or a comma. ("Quotation." "Quotation,") Close before semicolon or colon. ("Quotation"; "Quotation":)

Ordinarily, quotation marks are not required to enclose indented material unless indented material continues beyond one page. The indenting itself serves to punctuate the quotation. Note, however, that under some court rules quotation marks are required for indented quotations.

Use a single quotation mark to indicate quoted word or phrase within a quotation.

> As stated by the court, "Plaintiff's request for this relief is a 'red herring.' "

(j) Use of the Apostrophe

(1) Use an Apostrophe to Reflect Possession

Add apostrophe plus "s" or apostrophe alone.

Woman's   everyone's

Men's   Justices'

If a singular word ends in "s" and if an "s" would make it hard to pronounce, simply add an apostrophe. The apostrophe is usually added if the syllable is pronounced as in "goodness's," but not in "for goodness' sake."

To show joint or individual possession in a series of nouns or pronouns, use the apostrophe in the following manner:

Joint: "Williams, Green, and Mucklestone's policy" (the policy of the group or firm)

"Shannon, Forest, and Kassandra's property" (their joint property)

Individual: "Shannon's, Forest's, and Kassandra's policies" (each has separate policy or policies)

Do not use an apostrophe for possessives of personal pronouns: his, hers, theirs, ours, yours, its, whose.

(2) Use "Its" When You Need the Possessive Form of "It"

Perhaps the most frequent of all writing errors is the mistaken use of "its" for "it's" and vice versa. "Its" is a possessive, meaning "belonging to it." "It's" is the contraction of the two words "it is." Although common, this error gives the appearance of either sloppiness or ignorance. The argument section in an appellant's brief, for example, began with this sentence:

There being no showing that the defendant exercised dominion or control over the alcohol in his car, it's mere presence in his unoccupied automobile was insufficient to establish his constructive possession of the alcohol.

The mispunctuation of "its" in this sentence may create an initial impression of carelessness that can affect the persuasiveness of the argument itself.

(3) Use an Apostrophe to Indicate Omission of Letters

it's (it is)

they're (they are)

who's (who is)

(4) Use an Apostrophe for Certain Plurals

Use an apostrophe to make the possessive of plurals ending in "s."

First form the plural. If the plural ends in "s," add an apostrophe. If it does not, add "s."

labor unions'	years'
lawyers'	Johnsons'
witnesses'	mice's

Use "s" to form plurals of words used as words, of letters used as letters, and of numbers:

1. How many "yea's" are there?

2. The "7's" in the receipt are blurred.

3. "Occur" has two "c's" but only one "r."

(5) Use "S: With Gerunds but Not With Participles"

Use "s" with gerunds (verbs converted to nouns ending in "ing"). Use no "s" with participles (verbs converted to adjectives ending in "ing"). Decide which one to use according to what you want to emphasize, the word ending in "ing" or the noun preceding it.

1. The judge's leaving the court provoked comment. (The gerund "leaving" is emphasized.)

2. The judge leaving the court provoked comment. (The judge is emphasized. "Leaving" is a participle modifying the noun "judge.")

3. The court's holding in *Patner* set an important precedent. (The holding is emphasized)

4. The court holding in *Patner* set an important precedent. (The court is emphasized.)

(k) Use of the Exclamation Point

Unless an exclamation point occurs in a direct quotation, it should not be used by legal writers. It is rarely appropriate for professional writing of any kind.

Writers tend to use exclamation points to intensify or emphasize a point or idea. Rather than use an obvious, mechanical device, such as an exclamation point or underlining, select emphatic verbs and nouns.

(1) Use of Brackets

Brackets have the three following uses in legal writing. Use brackets to comment within a direct quotation:

"Provision for a joint and survivor annuity is required beginning on the date the employer reaches the earliest retirement age [*i.e.*, age 50] or ten years prior to normal retirement age [*i.e.*, 65 minus 10 = 55]."

Do not use brackets casually, however, to tailor quotations to fit your sentences. Design your sentences to fit grammatically and thematically with the quoted material.

Use brackets to indicate change of lower or upper case in the first letter of a direct quotation:

1. "[T]he site of the Company headquarters is the primary jurisdiction."

2. The booklet states that "[f]or a proper understanding of the Plan, the complete text should be read."

Use brackets to enclose a parenthetical expression inside parentheses:

She fails to cite the only relevant section of ERISA (assuming that ERISA [section 205(b)] will govern).

(m) Use of Ellipsis Points

Three points signal omission of a word or words in a quotation. *"Give me liberty or ... death."*

Do not begin a quotation with ellipsis points. Rather, use on of the following alternatives.

1. The Court held that the defendant "did not satisfy the conditions of the contract."

2. "[L]egal writers have a difficult audience: overworked judges."

Indicate omission of language from the end of a sentence by an ellipsis between the last word quoted and the final punctuation. In the following example, the fourth point is the sentence period.

Full sentence: "A board of directors selected by vote of the shareholders shall have the authority to discharge for sufficient cause all certificated and uncertificated employees according to the bylaws of the corporation."

With Ellipsis: A board of directors "shall ... discharge for sufficient cause all certificated and uncertificated employees...."

If a fully quoted sentence is followed by ellipsis, four periods are used. The first period is simply the normal sentence period. The remaining three periods are the usual ellipsis points.

"Readability is always lessened by long sentences.... [L]ong paragraphs also tire the reader."

(Ellipsis here means that words at the beginning of the second sentence have been omitted. If the capital "L" were not bracketed, omission of a full sentence would be indicated.)

If one or more entire paragraphs are omitted, use four points and indent them. Then begin the next paragraph on the next line. If the first word in a second or subsequent paragraph is omitted, show the omission by indenting three points. If a quotation begins in mid-paragraph, simply begin at the indented margin without ellipsis.

When typing, leave a space before the first ellipsis point and after the last. If an ellipsis follows a complete sentence, however, then the sentence period is placed immediately after the last letter of the last word in the sentence. For example, "Readability is always lessened by long sentences...."

(n) Punctuation of Citations

Citation sentences begin with capitals and end with periods. Citation clauses are set off from the rest of the text by a comma. Citations in a "string" are separated from one another by semi-colons. (See the "Blue Book," *A Uniform System of Citation,* for correct punctuation of introductory signals.)

(*o*) **Use of Italics**

Underlining is used in typewritten or handwritten work to show italics.

Use italics for foreign words and phrases unless they have been anglicized (*joie de vivre*, but not tortilla).

Use italics for the following Latin words and phrases, when used in legal writing. (Most other Latin words and phrases commonly used in legal writing are presumed to have been incorporated into the language of the law, thus are not underlined.)

qua	*quaere*
infra	*semble*
inter alia	
(alios)	
inter se (sese)	*sub nom.*
passim	*supra*

Use italics for signals used to introduce citations of authority:

E.g.,	*But see*
Accord	*But cf.*
See	*See generally*
Cf.	*See also*
Compare . . .	*Contra*
With . . .	

"See" is not underlined if it is part of an introductory textual phrase, however, as in, "For a discussion of the tortious interference rule, see *Restatement (Second) of Torts* § 766A and comments (1978)."

Use italics for names of cases, books, periodical articles, newspapers, ships, and aircraft (when used in text; the rule for use in footnotes may differ):

Spectre v. Bond, 107 F. Supp. 70 (D. Mass.1972)

New York Times

Princess Marguerite

Columbia

Use italics sparingly for words or phrases the writer wishes to emphasize. Italics or underlining for emphasis must not be used routinely, or all effect will be lost.

1. We are not concerned with *opinions* but with *facts*.

2. Washington's strong public policy against punitive damages should *not* be subordinated to other state policies.

The most common use of underlining for emphasis is inside quotations, for example:

Payment does not begin until Retirement Date; that date is the *later of* (1) date of entitlement or (2) month following 6–month absence for medical reasons.

(p) Use of Numerals and Section Symbols

In text, spell out the numbers zero to ninety-nine. In footnotes, spell out the numbers zero to nine. Use numerals for numbers over ninety-nine in text and for numbers over nine in footnotes.

Always spell out a number that begins a sentence.

Spell out round numbers like "thousand," "million," "hundred," if you wish. Simply be consistent.

If numbers over and under 100 occur in a series, use numerals for all. Items in a series containing only numbers under 100 should be spelled out.

Numerals should be used consistently for section numbers or other subdivision numbers, for percentages or dollar amounts, and for numbers containing a decimal point.

Leave one space between the section symbol (§) and the numeral: 18 U.S.C. § 2482.

Leave no space between the dollar sign and the numerals ($5.00) and the percentage sign and the numerals (7%).

If a symbol begins a sentence, write the word for the symbol out in full, for example, "Section 2482 was added in 1972." Do not begin a sentence with a symbol.

(q) Punctuation of Structured Enumeration

Introduce an enumerated series with a colon. If the elements of the series are incomplete sentences, use no initial capitalization and punctuate with semicolons or commas or omit punctuation.

§ 6.3   GRAMMAR

The basic components of English grammar are illustrated in a series of diagrams at the end of this section ("A Microgrammar").

(a) Subject–Verb Agreement

Verbs agree in number and person with the subject. The key to assuring agreement is to find the true subject and to determine whether it is singular or plural.

(1) Beware of Phrases Between Subject and Verb

Phrases coming between subject and verb do not affect the verb's form. Look for the true subject, especially where prepositional phrases come between subject and verb.

1. *One* of plaintiff's arguments *is* enough.

2. *Not one* of the witnesses *remembers* what happened.

3. *Principles of Medical Ethics*, published by the American Medical Association, *contains* provisions concerning confidential information.

(2) Beware of Lengthy Subject Phrases or Clauses

Agreement problems often occur where lengthy subject phrases or clauses separate subjects and verbs.

1. *Incorrect*: Washington's interest-analysis approach to choice of law problems result in the following holdings.

Corrected: Washington's interest-analysis approach to choice of law problems results in the following holdings.

2. *Incorrect*: The purpose for which a corporation may be organized under the current laws are "any lawful purpose or purposes, except for the purpose of banking."

Corrected: The purpose for which a corporation may be organized under the current laws is "any lawful purpose or purposes, except for the purpose of banking."

3. *Incorrect*: The correct use of quotation marks, enumeration, and a few other technical devices are briefly covered below.

Correct: The correct use of quotation marks, enumeration, and a few other technical devices is briefly covered below.

(3) *Use a Plural Verb With Most Compound Subjects*

1. A plumber and a pipefitter make more money than an English teacher.

2. Cars and one truck were trapped on the stranded ferry.

If the compound subject stands for a single unit, use a singular verb:

Finesse, Wrangle, and Pinch is a respectable firm.

If the compound subject consists of singular words joined by "or" or "nor," use a singular verb:

If oral ridicule or a written statement to a third person causes a person to be shunned or avoided, it may be defamatory.

Plural subjects joined by "or" or "nor" take plural verbs:

If neither written statements to a third party nor instances of oral ridicule cause a person to be shunned or avoided, then they are not defamatory.

If a singular subject and a plural subject are joined by "or" or "nor," make the verb agree with the nearer one:

If written statements to a third party or oral ridicule causes a person to be shunned or avoided, then there may be defamation.

(4) Use Singular Verbs With Most Indefinite Pronouns and Collective Nouns

Singular verbs may be used with the following pronouns and nouns:

all	every	nobody
another	everybody	someone
anything	everyone	something
each	everything	such a
each one	many a	
either	neither	

A few of these may be singular or plural depending on intended meaning: all, any, none, some, each, group, audience, committee, crowd.

In conversation, plural pronouns are frequently used to refer to singular nouns or pronouns, for example, "Everyone wants to have their efforts praised." This commonly occurs when people try to avoid using the singular pronouns "his" or "her." Nevertheless, in formal writing, subject-verb agreement should be precise and accurate.

Mass nouns take a singular verb unless they clearly have a plural meaning.

aesthetics	logistics	politics
economics	news	

(5) Make Forms of "to be" and Linking Verbs Agree With the Subject

A linking verb agrees with the subject, not the complement:

1.   The source of the funds is the property sale and the liquid assets.

2.   The property sale and the liquid assets are the source of the funds.

When forms of "to be" or verbs of being follow "there," they agree with the subject following:

1.   There are dozens of unconvincing arguments.

2.   There is no reason to try this case.

(b) Use of "Who" and "Whom"

Use the pronoun "who" when it will serve as a subject. Use the pronoun "whom" when it will serve as an object. In writing, the distinction should be carefully observed. In conversation, many people use "who" instead of "whom" because "whom" sounds unnatural or too formal. Most English speakers continue, however, to use "whom" in conversation whenever it follows a preposition–sometimes correctly, as in "You know of whom I spoke" "or give it to whom you like" or incorrectly, as in "The letter was lost by whomever received it."

In a few instances, determining the function of a relative pronoun may be difficult. Whether a relative pronoun serves as a subject or as an object is determined by its use in its own clause, not by whether its antecedent serves as a subject or as an object. For example, in "We know the ones who pay the bills," the relative pronoun's antecedent is "ones," which is the object of "know." Rather than using "whom," which serves as an object, the writer must use "who" because "who" is the subject of its own clause ("who pays the bills"). The entire clause "who pays the bills" stands in apposition to "ones."

1. We know *who* you are. (With this potentially confusing structure, "who" appears to serve both subject and object functions. However, if you ask "*what* do we know," then the answer becomes clear: We know "who you are." "Who you are" is a clause in which "who" is the subject-form following the linking verb "are." The object of the sentence is the entire unit "who you are.")

But: We know of *whom* you speak.

2. Checks were made of applicants who the landlord felt might not have been "congenial" tenants. ("Who" is the subject of the clause "who might not have been.").

But: Checks were made of applicants about *whom* the landlord had doubts.

3. Ask *who* the judge will be. (Here "who" is the subject-form following the verb "will be." The case must agree on either side of a linking verb, that is, subject and subject complement must be in the same case. Since "judge" is the subject, "who" must be used instead of "whom.")

But: Whom shall we ask to determine who the judge will be?

4. Mr. Throgmorton has been described as an oyster of the old school, *whom* nobody can open. ("Whom" is the object of the verb "can open.")

But: Mr. Throgmorton, *who* has been described as an oyster of the old school, cannot be opened.

(c) Use of Personal Pronouns

Whenever the first person pronoun replaces the subject, it must be "I." Whenever the first person pronoun replaces the object, it must be "me." Errors commonly occur when two or more pronouns are used together or when normal sentence order is inverted.

1. *Incorrect*: The trial was scheduled at the convenience of Ms. Buffum, Mr. Field, and I.

Correct: The trial was scheduled at the convenience of Ms. Buffum, Mr. Field, and me.

2. *Correct*: He thought the witness was I. (Not: "was me")

3. *Correct*: It is I.

4. *Correct*: The court can read the record as well as we. (To decide, simply fill in the missing words "as well as we can.")

Whenever the third person singular pronoun replaces the subject, it must be "he" or "she."

Whenever the third person singular pronoun replaces the object, it must be "him" or "her."

1. This is she. ("She" is the subject complement and must make sense on either side of "is," thus "she is she," not "her is she.")

2. It was *he* who argued. (Not: It was *him* who argued.)

3. It was *they* who requested the postponement. (Not: It was *them* who requested the postponement.)

4. Mr. Gann thought her to be *me*. (To test this, reverse "me" and "her." "Thought *me* to be *her*," not "thought *I* to be *her*.")

(d) Use of Reflexive Pronouns

The reflexive pronouns are myself, yourself, ourselves, herself, himself, and themselves. Reflexive pronouns have two uses: to reflect back on an agent (The *witness* perjured *himself*) and to emphasize something already named *(I myself* wrote the brief).

Do not use reflexive pronouns instead of personal pronouns.

1. *Incorrect*: Ms. Blumhagen and *myself* took the depositions.

Correct: *Ms. Blumhagen and I* took the depositions.

2. *Incorrect*: The document was signed by Mr. Ross and *myself*.

Correct: The document was signed by *Mr. Ross and* me.

(e) Which to Use: "Who," "Which," or "That"

"Who" or "whom" is used to refer to a person.

She is the lawyer *whom* I mentioned.

He is the one *who* ran for office.

"Which" is used to refer to everything except a person.

The evidence, *which* he misplaced, would have resolved the case.

We had never seen golden pheasants, *which* are more brilliantly plumed than parrots.

"That" is used to refer to either persons or things.

> She is the representative *that* I mentioned.

> We had never seen the golden pheasants *that* Mr. Fred Ellis raised.

(f) Pronoun Reference

(1) *Avoid Pronoun Confusion by Using Proper Names or by Repeating the Antecedent*

Meaning is more important here than "elegant variation."

> *Confusing*: The servant's liability stems from the duty owed to a *third person* under the law to conduct *himself* so as not to injure others.

> *Clear*: the servant's liability stems from the duty owed to a third person under the law requiring the servant to act so as not to injure others.

(2) *Avoid the Indefinite use of "It"*

The use of "it" in legal writing causes more confusion than any other pronoun reference. Avoid "it" whenever possible.

> *Confusing*: In this case , it is sought to carry forward, as it were, an anterior negligent omission of the defendants, though continuing, it is true, up to the time of the occurrence, and to assign to it the whole blame for the occurrence although by no effort of the defendants or of their servants could it at that stage have been prevented.

> *Clearer*: In this case, plaintiff seeks to carry forward an anterior negligent omission of the defendants that continued up to the time of the injury and to assign to the omission the whole blame for the injury, although

by no effort of the defendants or of their servants could the injury at that stage have been prevented.

Avoid phrases like "found it advisable." As Lewis Carroll demonstrates in Alice in Wonderland, this can be confusing:

"The patriotic archbishop of Canterbury found it advisable—"

"Found what?" said the Duck.

"Found it," the Mouse replied rather crossly: "Of course you know what 'it' means."

"I know what 'it' means well enough, when I find a thing," said the Duck. "It's generally a frog, or a worm. The question is, what did the archbishop find?"

(g) Use of Sex–Linked Pronouns

Many readers object to the use of masculine pronouns to indicate both sexes. Writers, on the other hand, have difficulty replacing them. When you face this problem, first try to avoid using any pronoun. If this approach will not work in a particular situation, try to change a singular pronoun to a plural.

1. *With pronoun:* A taxpayer may obtain a refund from the IRS by amending her returns for 1976, 1977, and 1978.

Without pronoun: A taxpayer may obtain a refund from the IRS by amending returns for 1976, 1977, and 1978.

2. *With pronouns*: A witness may be able to complain of nuisance even though the chemical plant has a dust easement on his or her property.

With plural pronoun: Witnesses may be able to complain of nuisance even though the chemical plant has a dust easement on their property.

If a singular pronoun must be used, the "he or she" form is preferable to either "he" or "she" alone. Although using "he or she," "his or hers," and "him or her" adds extra words and may be clumsy, it is usually accurate.

On printed forms, the use of "she/he" and "his/her" allows the individual user to cross out the inappropriate choice. The odd-looking "s/he" may save time in writing informal memoranda, but it should not appear in formal legal writing.

The third-person pronoun "one" may also be used to avoid the "he or she" problem. The pronoun "one," however, carries a formal tone, sometimes even a pompous tone, as in "One can hardly imagine oneself making such an argument." A few rare phrases are improved by replacing "man" with "one." The sentence "No man should trespass on another man's property" becomes "No one should trespass on another's property." Few opportunities of this kind, other than in statute drafting, are available to legal writers. Regardless of the solution found to the sex-linked pronoun dilemma, wording should be consistent within the same piece of work.

(h) Use of Subjunctive Mood

Although the subjunctive mood is disappearing from English, it still may be used to indicate a supposed, imagined, contingent, or nonfactual action or state.

> If her lawyer had succeeded, they would not now be bankrupt.

If settlement were possible, I would agree to it.

Whether the case be won or lost, we will get our fee.

Compare these forms of indicative and subjunctive:

Indicative	*Subjunctive*
I am; you are	If I be; If you be
I was; he was	If I were; If he were
I will be	If I should be
I will have been	If I should have been

§ 6.4   A MICROGRAMMAR

Diagrams for grammatical analysis are visual aids to understanding sentence structure. The following diagrams reflect a conventional method of "mapping" parts of speech. Reviewing these diagrams should assist writers in identifying the true Subject, Verb, and Object in their sentences. Only with a clear understanding of Subjects, Verbs, and Objects and how they interrelate can a writer produce clear and direct sentences.

A MICROGRAMMAR

1. Simple Sentence

    a. Subject and Predicate:

       i. Cars disappear.

<u>cars</u>	<u>disappear</u>
Subject	Verb

ii.   Court decided.

court	**decided**
Subject	Verb

b.   Subject and Predicate with Adverb and Adjective:

i.   Race cars disappear swiftly

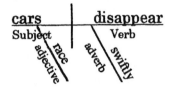

ii.   Trial court decided carefully

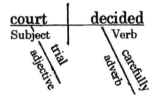

c.   Subject and Predicate with Prepositional Phrases:

i.   An antique car from Bellingham will win the race with a record time.

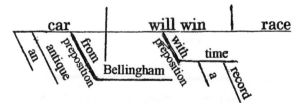

    ii.   The lower court in a similar case decided directly from the bench.

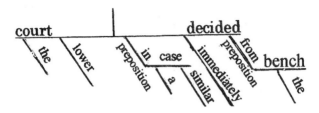

   d.   Subject, Predicate, Object, and Subjective Complement:

     i.   Court decided the case

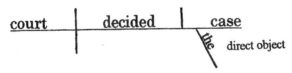

    ii.   Race cars are expensive

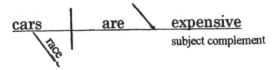

   e.   Compound Subject, Verb, Object

     i.   The Plaintiff and the Defendant settled the case

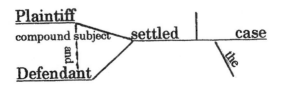

ii. The Plaintiff filed a stipulation and moved
     to dismiss the case.

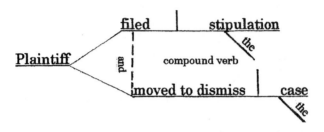

iii. The Plaintiff brought a claim for damages
      and a separate claim for injunctive relief.

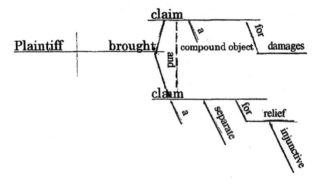

2. Compound Sentence

Race cars disappear, and flags fly.

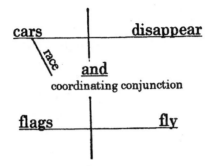

3. Complex Sentence

i. The race will continue unless the rain ruins the track.

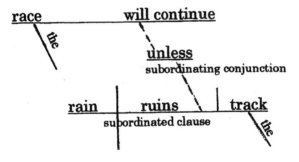

ii. Until the motion is heard, the court will not rule.

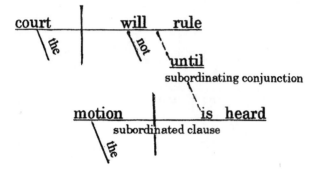

CHAPTER 7
INDIVIDUAL WRITING ANALYSIS

§ 7.1 INDIVIDUAL WRITING ANALYSIS

This method of analyzing an individual writing style was developed to help practicing attorneys improve their writing. The exercise is designed to identify the habits of an individual writer based on a 500–word writing sample. For the exercise to work, the writer must choose a typical sample, not an unusually well crafted one or an unusually poor one. Ideally, the writing sample will be from the discussion section of a legal memorandum or the analysis section of a brief. To begin, select a 500–word writing sample (roughly two typed pages) that reflects your normal, substantive writing style. Use a worksheet to record your analysis. A sample worksheet is shown below.

Step One: Count the number of sentences and the total number of words.

See Chapter 4 for instructions for counting words. Divide the number of words by the number of sentences in order to find the average number of words per sentence. Record this average on your worksheet. Count the number of sentences containing 35 or more words. Count the number of sentences containing fewer than six words.

As discussed in Chapter 4, the average sentence length for legal writing should be 20–25 words per sentence. This is longer than the recommended sentence length for general expository writing because legal writing is inherently more detailed than other forms of writing.

If your average sentence length is longer than 25 words per sentence, then you should practice the techniques for shortening sentences discussed in Chapter 4.

If more than 25% of your sentences contain 35 or more words, then you need to focus on sentence division, as described in Chapter 4. If you have no sentences with six or fewer words, then you should try using this technique for adding emphasis and increasing readability.

Step Two: Identify and count the types of sentences in your sample. For samples of each type of sentence, see Chapter 4. The grammatical diagrams at the end of Chapter 6 may also be helpful. Your worksheet should show the number and percentage of:

(1) simple sentences (one subject, one predicate)

(2) compound sentences (two or more sets of subjects and predicates joined by a coordinating conjunction)

(3) complex sentences (at least one subordinate clause in addition to a subject and predicate)

(4) sentences containing compound subjects, verbs, or objects (these may be compound or complex sentences)

Although there are no fixed guidelines for the percentages of types of sentences, at least 50% of your sentences should be simple in structure. The rest should primarily be complex, with few using the compound structure. A compound sentence can usually be converted to two simple sentences to enhance clarity and increase readability.

If you find that more than half of your sentences contain compound subjects, verbs, or objects, you should experiment with pairs of the appropriate subjects and verbs in separate sentences.

Step Three*:* Identify the structural pattern or "voice" of your sentences. Count the number of sentences written in the active and passive voice:

(1) Subject–Verb–Object pattern (active voice)

(2) Object–Verb–Subject (stated or implied) pattern (passive voice)

For each use of passive voice, identify the actor or agent. Determine the reason for removing or subordinating the actor or agent. For a review of active and passive voice, see Chapter 4.

Step Four: For each sentence, count the number of words that separate the Subject and the Verb. Divide by the number of sentences to find the averages. Count the number of sentences in which the Subject and Verb are separated by 7 or more words. Repeat these counts and calculations for Verbs and Objects.

For readability, no more than 7 to 10 words should separate the key parts of speech in a sentence, that is, the subject and verb (or predicate) and the verb and object. For further discussion, see Chapter 4.

Step Five: Count the number of sentences containing negative statements. Count any double negative structures, for example, "not without reason." Determine the percentage of sentences containing one or more negative statements or structures. Whenever possible, write in positive terms. Avoid double negatives, which slow your reader's comprehension and may be misread.

Step Six: Chart the sequence of sentences to check rhythm and variety. List the sentence lengths in the order that they appear. Look to see if the lengths are varied.

Step Seven: Count and identify the number and type of sentence "openers," that is, phrases that precede the true subject of the sentence. Transitional words, such as "however" or "therefore," do not count as non-sentence openers. Identify the types of non-subject sentence openers. Divide the total number of non-subject sentence openers by the number of sentences to find the percentage. Ideally, for maximum readability, 75% of sentences should open with the subject. Thus, the percentage of non-subject openers should not exceed 25%. Very short and simple opening prepositional phrases, such as "In the preceding appeal,'' do not lessen readability significantly unless they are used frequently. Find:

(1) % of subject openers

(2) % of prepositional phrases as openers

(3) % of adverbial phrases as openers

(4) % of adjectival phrases as openers

(5) % of other parts of speech used as openers

Step Eight: Identify any dangling modifiers. Check all modifying phrases by locating the noun or verb that they modify. Note any modifiers that are ambiguous, that is, that could modify more than one word or phrase. Note any nonsensical modifiers. See Chapter 4 for examples.

Step Nine: Paragraph Analysis:

(1) Count the number of paragraphs.

(2) Count the number of words in each paragraph.

(3) List the numbers of words per paragraph in the order that the paragraphs occur to check for variety of paragraph length.

(4) Calculate the average number of words per paragraph. If the average number of words per paragraph exceeds 150, you should find ways of shortening some paragraphs.

(5) Identify the reason for each paragraph break: logical division, rhetorical effect, or visual ef-

fect. If you have no rhetorical or visual paragraph breaks, try using them for emphasis.

(6) Identify the topic sentences in each paragraph. Count the number of paragraphs that begin with the topic sentence. Ninety percent of your paragraphs should begin with the topic sentence. For those paragraphs that do not open with the topic, identify the reason for delaying it. Is the reason sufficient given the reader's expectation and need to know the topic immediately?

(7) Evaluate the first and last sentences of each paragraph. Do they deserve to be in positions of greatest emphasis?

(8) Underline transitional words and phrases. Are there enough transitions to move the reader smoothly from sentence to sentence and from idea to idea? Are the appropriate transitional words used? For additional transitional words, see Chapter 2.

Step Ten: Punctuation:

(1) Count the number of interruptions resulting from sets of commas, sets of parenthesis, sets of brackets, and sets of dashes. Calculate the average number of interruptions per sentence. For greatest readability, this percentage should be kept below 50%.

(2) Notice any mark of punctuation that recurs. Do you tend to use semicolons to separate units of thought? Could you use periods and

transitional words instead? Do you tend to use dashes to slow the reader down? Would more careful word choice accomplish the same goal more effectively?

Step Eleven: Language:

(1) Count the number of verbs that denote action ("transitive" verbs like "run") and the number of times that forms of "to be" occur. Writing with specific active verbs rather than forms of "to be" will strengthen and clarify your writing. At least two-thirds of your verbs should be active verbs.

(2) Count the number of adjectives and adverbs. Calculate the number of adjectives and adverbs per sentence. If you have more than 100%, experiment with deleting them. Use stronger verbs and nouns to avoid the tendency to add unneeded modifiers. Adjectives and adverbs sometimes weaken the nouns and verbs that they modify; thus removing them can strengthen a sentence.

Step Twelve: Wordiness and Redundancy:

As an exercise, strike through 100 words in your writing sample. Eliminate each word that is not essential. Eliminate all redundancy, even if it serves a rhetorical purpose. The point of this exercise is to identify your individual tendencies to wordiness. Print out your 400–word writing sample and ask someone to compare it with the original. Which is easier to read? Which communicates more clearly? How much substance has been lost? Does it matter?

§ 7.2 **WRITING ANALYSIS WORKSHEET**

1. Total number of sentences ___
    Total Number of words ___
    Average words per sentence ___
    Number of sentences with 35 words or more ___
    Number of sentences with 6 words or fewer ___

2. Number of simple sentences ___
    % of simple sentences ___
    Number of compound sentences ___
    % of compound sentences ___
    Number of complex sentences ___
    % of complex sentences ___
    Number of sentences with compound subjects, verbs, or objects ___

3. Number of sentences in Active Voice ___
    Number of sentences in Passive Voice ___
    % of sentences in Active Voice ___
    % of sentences in Passive Voice ___
    Reasons for use of Passive voice: _____

4. Number of words separating subjects and verbs ___
    Average number of separating words per sentence ___
    Number of sentences with more than 7 words separating the subject and verb ___
    Number of words separating verbs and objects ___

Average number of separating words per sentence ___

Number of sentences with more than 7 words separating the verb and object ___

5. Number of sentences with negative statements ___

   % of sentences with negative statements ___

6. List sentence lengths in the order they occur.
   Check for variety of sentence length.

7. Number of sentences that open with their subject ___

   Number of sentences that do not open with their subject ___

   % of sentences that open with their subject ___

   Number and % of prepositional phrases used to open sentences ___

   Number and % of adverbial or adjectival phrases used to open sentences ___

   Number and % of other parts of speech used to open sentences ___

8. List any dangling or ambiguous modifiers (see Chapter 4).

9. Count the number of paragraphs ___

   Calculate the average number of words per paragraph ___

   Count the number of words in each paragraph separately, then list the numbers in the order that the paragraphs occur to check for variety of paragraph length.

10. Identify the reason for each paragraph break (see Chapter 2).

    Number and % of logical breaks _____

    Number and % of rhetorical breaks _____

    Number and % of visual breaks _____

11. Identify the topic sentence in each paragraph.

    Number and % of paragraphs beginning with topic sentence _____

    Reasons for placing topic sentences in the middle or at the end:

12. Check the first and last sentences of each paragraph. Are these positions of emphasis used effectively?

13. Locate all transitional words and phrases. Do they provide logical links between all sentences and paragraphs?

14. Count the number of sentence interruptions caused by commas, parentheses, brackets, dashes, or internal citations ____.

    Calculate the average number of interruptions per sentence ____

15. Number and % of semi-colons per sentence
    _____

    Number and % of dashes per sentence _____

    Number and % of any other frequently used punctuation mark

    per sentence _____

16. Number and % of active verbs per sentence
    _____

Number and % of forms of "to be" per sentence

_____

17. Number and % of adjectives per sentence

_____

Number and % of adverbs per sentence _____

Note: if the percentages are 100% or greater, try reducing your use of adjectives and adverbs.

18. Omit 100 words in your writing sample. Print the shorter version. Which version is clearer? Which is easier to read? Ask a friend to compare the two versions.

CHAPTER 8

RESEARCH MEMORANDA AND CLIENT LETTERS

§ 8.1 INTRODUCTION

This chapter discusses two basic forms of advisory writing, letters to clients and office research memoranda. It introduces the problems of communicating with lay persons and suggests techniques for solving those problems. It explains special features of office memoranda and suggests techniques for writing them. Finally, this chapter suggests ways of combining these techniques with those described in preceding chapters.

§ 8.2 WRITING FOR A LAY AUDIENCE

Lawyers write to clients to give answers to legal questions and to describe possible courses of action and attendant risks. Most clients are lay persons, that is, they do not have special knowledge of the law, its concepts, and its terminology. Because the lawyer should write for the client's benefit and understanding, writing an advisory letter to a client can be a difficult writing task. The first step is to recognize the problem.

Before beginning to write a letter to a client, ask these questions: What can I assume this client knows? Can I assume some or no acquaintance with the law? How can I accommodate legal language and writing style to this reader without sounding condescending?

Write the letter with the answers to those questions and with the following guidelines constantly in mind:

Be direct. Answer the client's questions directly and give advice or recommendations within the first few sentences. If direct answers and advice cannot be given, say so, and explain why. If you cannot provide an answer, admit it. Do not try to bluff.

Be complete. State completely any advice or recommendations for action. State the facts upon which you base your answers and advice. This will allow your client to judge whether you are acting on complete and accurate information.

If the purpose of the letter is to weigh risks or courses of action, as in litigation, then consider theories of liability, possible damages, and probability of winning. Both the client's case and the opposing case should be outlined and fairly evaluated. Give reasons in language the client can understand.

Be clear. Use plain language instead of technical terms. That is more difficult than may at first appear. In 1977 the New York legislature adopted a "plain language" law requiring clarity in form contracts used in consumer transactions. Many other state legislatures have now adopted similar laws requiring that such contracts be clearly written with commonly used words and appropriate sections and headings. However, the plain language crusade has met with resistance among some lawyers because it is not possible to write all legal documents plainly enough for all persons to understand. Nevertheless, the plain language movement has led to general agreement in the legal profession that documents such as mortgage and insurance forms should be understandable to the lay reader.

A lawyer's letter to a lay client should also be written in plain language. The following principles, developed as a part of the plain language movement, may aid in reaching that end:

(i) Words and phrases with which a lay reader is probably unfamiliar should be replaced with familiar words whenever this may be done without loss of meaning. For example, instead of "voir dire," write "questioning of prospective jurors." Instead of "statute of frauds," write "a statute that requires some contracts to be written."

(ii) Technical terms and terms of art should be defined or illustrated or both. If a definition would be too complex and difficult for a lay reader, an example should be used instead.

(iii) Terms with both legal and common meanings (for example "privilege") should be avoided or the differing meanings should be clearly identified.

(iv) To write plainly about the law, legal writers may sometimes have to sacrifice brevity, as in the examples given above for the first guideline.

Be specific. Give exact times, costs, and other important information whenever possible. If exact information cannot be provided, explain why, and state when it will or may be available.

Be brief when the subject matter permits. Short letters need no apology. Do not pad a short letter. Omit legal analysis that does not directly explain your answer. Omit unnecessary expressions, such as "I would like to inquire about" (just inquire) and "we regret to inform you that" (just inform).

Be realistic. Unless you are writing a formal opinion letter, leave out case analysis, obscure statutory language, and citations of authority. Of course, some clients may want this information as the basis for evaluation of the lawyer's answer or for assurance of lawyer-like consideration of the problem. For most clients, however, citations will be indecipherable. Before including case analysis or citations of authority, ask yourself whether your client will want to have and will understand this information.

Be objective. Lawyers sometimes argue their cases in letters to clients as an unconscious "warm-up" exercise before addressing the court. Such argument may have the unhappy effect of leading a client to expect more than the lawyer can deliver. Advisory writing may be argumentative at times, but the argument should have a specific, defensible purpose (*i.e.*, to persuade a client to give up a law suit or to change settlement terms).

Be considerate. Your client is someone with a problem. Try to solve that problem in a sincere and humane way. This requires careful control of tone. Do not joke about the severity or the insignificance of the client's problems. Keep the same level of formality throughout the letter. Do not begin with "Dear Charlie" and close with "Very truly yours, Bickerstaff, Edgewater, and Ransom." Do not try to impress your clients by using a formal or pompous tone, obscure reasoning, difficult legal terms, or pompous phrases, such as "preposterous on its face," "with matters in this recumbent posture," "a date certain," and "purports to know." Your letterhead and bill will impress them enough.

EXAMPLES:

1. *Mixed tone (formal and colloquial)*: While no advantage to deletion of the provision is apparent, its deletion would not be the end of the world. I shall by separate cover provide for your perusal other illustrative provisions.

Revised: To omit the provision will do no harm that I can see. I will send other similar provisions to you in a separate letter. (Or: Next week I will send other similar provisions to you.)

2. *Wordy and indirect*: This will reply to your written inquiry of August 10, 2002, concerning certain aspects of your purchase. My delay in responding is due to overwhelming work for other clients. After extensive research, I am not able to consider the issues that you raise in the order that they occur in the letter.

Revised: In response to your August 10 inquiry, I have researched your problem and will answer your questions in the order you have asked them.

3. *Indirect*: The following discussion addresses a concern raised by Ms. McGuire during your recent claims review. It was suggested that some discrepancy might possibly exist.

Revised: During your recent claims review, Ms. McGuire suggested that a discrepancy exists.

4. *Stilted wording*: The following basic principles must be considered so that the rationale for careful utilization of medical records can be appreciated.

Note: Will the client want to "appreciate the rationale?"

Revised: Medical records must be used carefully for the following reasons.

5. *Mixed metaphors*: Give me a call when you have digested this letter, and we can move ahead with the next step.

Revised: Please call when you are ready to proceed.

§ 8.3 OFFICE RESEARCH MEMORANDA

(a) Purposes

The office research memorandum is the basic document used in law offices. Its general purpose is to provide an analysis of a problem as the basis for giving advice or making decisions about the problem.

A memorandum should be written to serve the specific purpose for which it is requested. For example, an attorney may request a memorandum as the basis for:

(i) Considering whether to accept a case;

(ii) Preparing to meet with the client to obtain additional facts about the client's problem;

(iii) Preparing to advise a client on which of several courses of action to take;

(iv) Preparing for negotiations with the client's adversary;

(v) Preparing to draft a settlement agreement or other contract;

(vi) Preparing to draft a pleading or a discovery document;

(vii) Preparing for trial; or

(viii) Preparing for an appeal or other review of a court decision.

Even though preparation for settlement, trial, or appeal may not be the immediate purpose for a memorandum request, the memorandum discussion may have to be written with these future possibilities in mind.

Usually a memorandum will be written for another lawyer, such as a senior partner or associate. Sometimes, however, memoranda will be written for or shared with other professionals, such as accountants or trust officers. The prospective readers and the specific purposes of a memorandum should be identified as early in the research and writing process as possible to permit development of a solution responsible to the audience and purposes.

(b) Writing the Questions Presented

(1) Introduction

Identification of questions presented by a legal problem is the key to effective analysis. Sometimes questions will be clearly and precisely identified by the person who requests a research memorandum. More often, precise identification comes slowly as a product of research, analysis of authorities, and reflective thinking.

Once questions are mentally identified, effective phrasing of them presents another challenge: how best to communicate the writer's understanding of the questions precisely and concisely to the reader. That is the subject of this subsection.

(2) Draft the Ultimate Question

To return to the beginning, think first about what we will call the "ultimate question," the general question that prompts the request for a memorandum. The ultimate question may be as general as this: Can our client be liable under any theory for failure to arrange for transfer of this fire insurance for the benefit of the buyer of the stadium that was later destroyed by fire? Or, it may be as specific as this: Whether evidence of plaintiff's remarriage is admissible in an action for wrongful death of a spouse. If the ultimate question is not clearly stated for you, try to draft a statement as soon as you begin work on a problem.

(3) Incorporate Key Facts

Questions should be meaningful standing alone. The readers should not have to read the full statement of facts in order to understand the questions. Questions will be meaningful if they are stated in terms of the facts of the problem, not phrased in the abstract. Compare the following abstract question with the questions stated in the preceding paragraph:

> Whether a promise to arrange for transfer of a fire insurance policy is enforceable.

If you use subquestions, each subquestion may incorporate the facts peculiarly significant to that subquestion. This practice will reduce the number of facts to be incorporated in the primary question. The questions should state facts and not legal conclusions.

Generally, when several facts are included in a single issue sentence, the law is stated before the facts. If the subject matter permits, the facts should be arranged from the most general to the most particular. The question itself should thus move from the general area of law, at the beginning, to the most particular fact, at the end.

The question should include only the key facts. Dates, amounts, locations, and other details would ordinarily not be necessary, since they will be supplied in a following Statement of Facts. If the key facts are numerous, a preliminary factual summary may be necessary to avoid an overlong question statement. For example:

Our client sold a stadium that was later destroyed by fire. The buyer alleges that at the time the sale was closed, our client promised to arrange for transfer of his fire insurance policy for the benefit of the buyer.

Question: May the client be liable to the buyer for the full loss for failing to perform the alleged promise?

(4) Use Subquestions Effectively

Formulation of more specific subquestions will often be necessary as research and analysis progress. Writing and rewriting these questions will often advance understanding of the problem and promote reasoning to reliable conclusions.

Ordinarily, the more specific the questions, the more clearly and precisely they can be discussed. A problem can be subdivided into so many specific questions, however, that both the reader and the writer become confused. Guard against possible confusion by asking whether your questions are related and whether the relationships are apparent. Guard against your reader's possible confusion by asking whether numerous subquestions will prevent a unified view of the problem.

The form and style of questions will vary with the subject matter, as illustrated by the examples in the preceding paragraphs of this section. Note, however, that a single subquestion is never used. If there is a subquestion "a," then there is a subquestion "b." The existence of at least two subquestions follows from the logic of division: If something is divided into parts, there must be at least two parts. When a primary question is stated with a single "subquestion," either the subquestion is a more specific restatement of the primary question or it is one of two or more subquestions. If you are tempted to state single subquestion, decide which you must do: substitute the more specific formulation for the primary question or identify and state the other parts of the whole.

(5) Revise

Expect to revise your issue statements several times, including a final revision when you have finished writing the entire memorandum. Many of the suggestions for revision of sentences appearing in Chapter 4 will be useful in revising questions statements.

(c) Writing the Brief Answer

This answer must be short. Answer each question in one sentence if possible. Cite precedents only if they are the crux of the problem. Although the Brief Answer appears before the Discussion section, it is often written after the Discussion section is in final or nearly final form. The clear understanding required for a succinct answer may come only after you have written a detailed Discussion.

(d) Writing the Statement of Facts

The Statement of Facts sets forth the basis of the legal problem. It tells the reader what happened, when, how, and to whom. No conclusions are reached. Editorial comments or evaluations of events are reserved for the Discussion section.

Facts should be presented so that the reader will understand on first reading and remember the key facts while reading the Discussion section. The facts should be stated in simple language without distortion or bias. The distinction between alleged facts and established facts should be observed through use of appropriate verbs, such as "alleged," "testified," "found by the court." Significant questions of fact should be signaled by mention of inconsistent information.

The two most common orders for fact statements are chronological and topical. Chronological order is most frequently used. The key facts are stated in the first sentence or two to orient the reader (that is, what happened, when, where, to whom). Then the events are narrated. Paragraphs in a chronological fact statement may be opened with relevant dates to make the chronology clear.

Topical order may be needed to organize a complex set of facts. Topic headings may then be used to identify shifts in topic. Be careful to introduce and conclude this type of fact summary and to provide explicit transitions and headings. Topical order is common for multi-party problems (for example, litigation involving several cross-claims or numerous defendants) requiring that relationships among the parties be discussed separately.

Many of the suggestions for revision of sentences that appear in Chapter 4 are useful in revising fact statements, as illustrated in the following example.

Unclear Statement of Facts:

The plaintiffs were general partners of a brokerage firm that was liquidated and its assets transferred to defendant Cheerios, a partnership, and as part of the transaction, Cheerios sold to plaintiffs general and limited partnership units of Cheerios. The plaintiffs alleged a violation by Cheerios of the antifraud provisions of the federal securities statutes, which violation resulted in plaintiffs having purchased their partnership interests for more than they were allegedly worth.

Revised and Clarified:

The plaintiffs were general partners of a brokerage firm that was liquidated.[1] The firm's assets were transferred to defendant Cheerios, also a partnership. As part of the transaction, Cheerios sold general and limited partnership units of Cheerios to the plaintiffs. The plaintiffs alleged that Cheerios violated[4] the antifraud provision of the federal securities statutes. They further alleged[5] that this violation resulted in their purchase of partnership interests for more than they were allegedly worth.

[1]One idea per sentence.

[2]Transitional words.

[3]Normal word order restored.

[4]Active, not passive, voice.

[5]Parallelism (fourth and fifth sentences).

(e) Writing the Discussion

(1) Write About the Particular Problem

A memorandum will usually be the basis for an attempt to resolve a particular dispute. Therefore, the law discussed should be clearly related to the particular facts of the dispute.

(2) *Express Your Analysis and Conclusions Objectively*

The purpose of an office memorandum is to explore the possible solutions to a legal problem. Exploration requires objectivity. The objective writer must explain the arguments that could be made for each side of the dispute and then assess their relative strengths.

The law student or beginning lawyer may have trouble writing objectively because the objective style is unfamiliar at first. All writers want to express feelings and opinions, especially if they have strongly held views. The process of researching and analyzing a problem often leads the researcher to strongly held opinions. One reason for this is that a legal problem usually requires inductive reasoning: the researcher gathers particulars in order to arrive at a generalization. Legal writing, however, generally requires a deductive format: the conclusion (generalization) is presented first, followed by statement of the analysis (contributing particulars). The use of deductive structure may cause the writer to try to prove favored generalizations and thus become argumentative. Memorandum writers must correct these argumentative tendencies if they are to lead the reader to an objective understanding of the problem.

(3) *Write With Your Reader in Mind*

For most office memoranda, the audience will be a lawyer. In this most common situation, you are speaking as a specialist to a specialist. Keep in mind, however, that you probably know more about the subject you have just researched than does the reader for whom you write. Provide the necessary background for understanding by explaining basic propositions and technical terms with which the reader may not be familiar or which the reader may not immediately recall.

In writing for a lawyer, a legal writer can take advantage of many shortcuts in communication. Legal terms of art and legal analysis will be readily understood, freeing the writer from detailed explanation. This license should not be abused, however, by using esoteric diction or jargon, by failing to provide logical connections between ideas because they seem "obvious," or by displaying high-sounding legal notions that are irrelevant to the subject.

If prospective readers are non-lawyers, then keep in mind the level of legal knowledge of the reader. Consider the suggestions about writing for lay persons that appear in the first section of this chapter.

(4) Be Conservative in Style and Tone

Express personal style primarily by sentence structures, not by idiosyncratic diction or by colloquialism. Colloquialism is easy to misinterpret and difficult to control in terms of tone and effect. A colloquial tone distracts from the information being conveyed. Avoid idiosyncratic expressions, such as "*early on* in the deposition," an "*outrageous* position," and "*on the order of* $110,000 in bonds."

The memorandum writer's tone should be unobtrusive so that the information is highlighted. A matter-of-fact tone is achieved by a straightforward, unequivocal declaration of findings and conclusions, without apologies or unnecessary qualifications.

(5) Be Selective in Using Quotations

Paraphrase judicial language rather than quoting at length. Isolate the relevant judicial language, quote it directly with necessary context, and paraphrase the rest. The reader should not have to decide what part of a long quotation is important.

(6) Use Headings and a Practical Format

The whole writing should be easy to use for quick reference. Divisions should be clearly marked. Sections should be easy to locate.

Topic headings should be used for major divisions of any legal document of more than two or three pages. Subheadings may also be used to identify the topic of a paragraph or block of paragraphs, thereby reinforcing the traditional topic sentence.

To write headings, remember the purposes to be served. Proper use of headings (i) assists the writer in organizing the document, (ii) assists the reader in understanding the writer's organization, (iii) assists the reader in referring back to matters covered in the document, (iv) assists the writer in making transitions between topics, and (v) informs the reader of a topic change.

Following are suggestions for form:

(i) Topic headings should be short to help the reader locate information quickly.

(ii) Form should be consistent: Use either complete sentences or topic summaries, but do not switch back and forth. The questions presented may be effective headings.

(iii) All words in fragmentary topic headings should begin with capital letters except prepositions (such as "of," "in"), articles (such as "a," "the"), and conjunctions of four letters or fewer (such as "and," "but").

(iv) Fragmentary topic headings are not punctuated.

(v) A colon is used for compound topic headings, for example: *The Basics: When Partition is Available.*

(vi) Headings are customarily underlined.

(f) Writing the Conclusion

The conclusion may be used to tie together the answers already expressed for several questions presented. It may be used to state recommendations for handling a matter. It should not be a repetition of the Brief Answer, but it may parallel the Brief Answer. For example, the conclusion may provide more detailed explanations of reasoning summarily stated in the Brief Answer. Whatever its content, it should summarize. It should not introduce new authorities or new information about authorities covered in the Discussion.

§ 8.4　THE FINAL TOUCH

As every experienced writer knows, the first draft is never good enough. Revision is essential. Even a short letter should be reviewed for clarity, for ease of reading, for conciseness, and for errors. Extensive memoranda or briefs should be revised or rewritten several times. If the client can afford only one draft, then the lawyer must draft with extra care and review that draft conscientiously. If the pressure of time prevents the original writer from revising, someone else should review the work. Revision should be done on a printed page, rather than on a computer screen in order to keep the whole document in mind.

Ideally, the work should be printed and put away for at least one day before revision. The lapse of time will allow the writer to return to the draft with greater detachment and a fresher eye.

During revision, the writer should review paragraphs and paragraph blocks to make sure that the topics are clearly indicated and well supported in the body of the paragraphs. The logical sequence of topics should be checked. The writer should review for adequate, informative transitions between paragraphs and sections. Sentences should be reviewed for readability and precision. For troublesome sentences, use the simple method for revision described in Chapter 4. After paragraphs and sentences have been re-examined, check for concise, parallel headings and subheadings. When writing on a computer or when dictating, it is especially important for the writer to see how paragraphs and sections look when printed.

As part of the revision, the writer should read the whole for uniform style and for consistency in wording and tone. Every citation and quotation should be checked against the original. Whenever possible, the writer should have someone else read for comprehensibility of sentences, usage, punctuation, and spelling. Although misspellings and typographical errors may provide comic relief to your reader, they do so at your expense. One lawyer learned just how expensive a typographical error can be after he signed and mailed a letter informing a prospective client that he would charge a "fat fee" (instead of a "flat fee").

All misspellings and mistypings are the responsibility of the author, not of the typist or the "spell-check" program. If you cannot replace an incompetent typist, learn to proofread your own work with extra care. If you have difficulty spelling correctly, keep a list of words that your regularly misspell at your desk when you write and have someone who spells correctly proofread your work.

CHAPTER 9

ARGUMENTATIVE MEMORANDA AND PERSUASIVE WRITING

§ 9.1 INTRODUCTION

This chapter explains special features of briefs and suggests techniques for presenting these features persuasively. The basis for discussion will be a brief for an appellate court. The suggestions also apply to argumentative briefs and memoranda prepared for trial and administrative judges, although the form, permissible length, and degree of formality may differ.

Brief writing is formal. The content, the format, the wording, and the writer's tone are all subject to conventions, discussed below. Appellate court rules provide detailed requirements for page size, length, necessary subdivisions, order of subdivision, general content, and covers (even the color may be prescribed). The Rules on Appeal of the United State Supreme Court are cited as the basis for many suggestions in this section. These rules are representative of other courts' requirements for appeal briefs as well. Remember, however, to consult the controlling rules before beginning to write any brief or argumentative memorandum.

§ 9.2 PREPARATION FOR WRITING

Preparation will begin with a review of the record of the case and of prior research on the legal issues. Tentative decisions must be made as to which facts in the record are significant and which legal arguments to use. Then the Argument section of the brief may be tentatively outlined, perhaps in the form of the logical series of contentions. Finally, decisions can be made about questions to be stated. After tentative identification of the questions, the record may be reviewed again one or more times before firm decisions are made about the questions and arguments to be presented.

A limited number of questions and arguments should be selected. In general, judges and other specialists on appellate advocacy agree that argument on numerous questions may detract from rather than enhance overall persuasiveness. Common advice is to argue the strongest points–perhaps only two or three–even though there are many attractive possibilities. These specialists suggest that if you cannot win on the strongest points, you should not expect to win on the weaker points; argument on many points may only annoy the judges. Of course, a case may be so complex that many questions must be argued, for example, if reversal can be justified only by favorable answers to numerous questions. Even in a complex case, however, questions can be related to each other and combined so as to reduce the number of questions normally stated as "Questions Presented." The following guidelines should help you to select the questions to argue:

(i) Prefer the strong points over the weak points.

(ii) Other things being equal,

    a.   prefer simple questions over complex questions, and

    b.   prefer related questions over unrelated questions.

The order of the discussion in the following sections should not be regarded as the necessary order for writing a brief. Where one begins in writing a brief depends on the nature of the case. The following discussion begins with the Questions Presented only because they appear first in Supreme Court brief form. The order of the remaining discussion also follows the Supreme Court's form.

§ 9.3 WRITING EFFECTIVE QUESTIONS

From the viewpoint of judges, the function of questions is to provide a quick picture of a case about which they know nothing. Questions must be written to serve that function. From the viewpoint of counsel, an additional function of questions is to provide the judges with a favorable picture of a case. Questions should therefore be written to serve that persuasive function—but without misleading or alienating the judges. That calls for skill and the touch of an artist.

The quick-picture function of questions is emphasized by the rules of the United States Supreme Court that place the Questions Presented first: before the Table of Contents, before the Statement of the Case, and before the other subdivisions required in a brief, in a petition for writ of certiorari (discretionary review), or in a jurisdictional statement (appeal as of right). Some other courts' rules also require that questions (or points or assignments of error) appear as one of the early subdivisions. Therefore, just as in a memorandum, the questions must be meaningful standing alone.

The Supreme Court rules require that the questions presented be expressed in terms of the circumstances of the case, but without unnecessary detail. The statements should be short and concise, but not argumentative or repetitious. The need to state questions using the circumstances of a case (that is, to incorporate key facts) rather than in abstract terms has been emphasized in Chapter 8 in the description of effective questions for memoranda. To say that questions should be short and concise and not repetitious is to state a fundamental rule of writing. That the questions should not be argumentative, however, may seem to conflict with counsel's goal to state questions that will persuade the judges to accept the counsel's viewpoint. Questions can be drafted to be persuasive, however, without being argumentative.

To write a persuasive question, you must state a question on which the outcome of the case depends and ask it in such a way that only one reasonable answer follows: yours. The facts to be included must be selected carefully for their persuasive value. The sentence itself must be rhetorically structured so as to emphasize the most favorable facts. The conclusion that the court is to reach should be implicit. All this must be done without distorting either the law or the facts and without appearing to be argumentative. Here are examples of effective questions written from opposing viewpoints.

Petitioner's question: Does Title VII of the Civil Rights Act of 1964 make unlawful a program adopted by an employer and a union in collective bargaining, which reserves for black bidders 50% of the openings in an in-plant training program in order to eliminate a racial imbalance in the skilled craft workforce?

Respondent's question: Whether under Title VII of the Civil Rights Act of 1964 an employer and a labor union may, solely in order to achieve a desired ratio of minority workers in craft positions at a manufacturing plant, institute a racial quota for admission to craft training programs in the absence of any prior discrimination against the minority workers at that plant?

Here, on the other hand is a question that is argumentative.

Whether under Title VII of the Civil Rights Act of 1964 an employer and a labor union may institute a racial quota for admission to training programs that is preferential to recently hired members of minority groups and discriminates against whites, who are thus deprived of rights to entry into training programs earned under job seniority acquired through years of labor.

Another ineffective type of question is the conclusory question, one that states the nature of the conclusion to be reached without giving a clue about the specific answer. For example, "The question is whether the complaint is legally insufficient." The desired conclusion should be implicit in the question, for example: "Is a complaint for breach of contract insufficient in law if it does not allege performance by the plaintiff or offer any excuse for her nonperformance?"

Questions Presented may be stated in either declarative form or question form ("The question is . . ." or "Whether . . .").

§ 9.4   WRITING THE STATEMENT OF THE CASE

(a) The Nature of the Case

The Statement of the Case consists primarily of a statement of the significant facts of the case. First, however, the legal scene must be set with a description of the nature of the proceeding if that is not stated before or as a part of the Questions Presented. The description should be a short paragraph that identifies the general subject of the case and how it was disposed of in the lower court.

> This is an action for damages for interference with an alleged contractual relationship. After trial before the court without a jury, judgment was entered against the defendants for $127,000.

A summary of additional procedural details may be necessary, but try to avoid a lengthy summary of procedural steps before the human side of the case is introduced. For example, first identify the parties (if your client might evoke a sympathetic attitude) or interweave the review of necessary procedural details with the narration of facts. (The governing rules may, however, require a separate summary of the pleadings and procedure.) Summarize only those procedural steps that are material to the questions to be argued or necessary to an understanding of the case.

(b) The Statement of Facts

How the facts are stated may be more important than the argument of law itself. Judges frequently advise lawyers to spend more time on facts and less time on legal arguments. The judges initially know nothing about the case. They want to know what happened, when, where, and to whom. Do not deaden this desire to know with an overly detailed or dry recital.

The facts must be candidly set forth, but the writer may arrange them, phrase them, and expand or condense treatment of particular events so as to emphasize favorable facts and to diminish unfavorable facts. Juxtaposition, placement within sentences and paragraphs, choice of verbs and nouns: all of these assist in presenting facts in a persuasive way.

Careful selection is the first step toward writing a persuasive fact statement. Both favorable and unfavorable facts must be included. Disputed and undisputed facts and alleged and established facts must be distinguished in order to establish the writer's credibility or ethical appeal. Only material facts should be included with the possible exception of substantively non-material details that add human interest or create the desired impression or context. Use of non-material details for this purpose, however must be limited and subtle. Visual details and direct conversation may be used to arouse the reader's interest and draw the reader into the event. Selection of all these kinds of human interest details should be carefully limited, however, to avoid unduly extending the statement of facts.

Careful arrangement is the second step toward a persuasive fact statement. Use a simple organizational pattern. Remember that the judges are not familiar with the facts. The judges will assimilate the facts more readily if they are stated in chronological order or in clearly defined topical order. If the fact statement is long, use headings to help the reader understand, relate, and remember the facts.

Careful presentation of facts is the third step toward a persuasive fact summary. The following suggestions should help you to set forth the facts clearly and favorably without distorting them.

Refer to parties as descriptively as possible. For example, use "husband" and "wife" in a domestic relations case; use "employer" and "employee" or "worker" in a labor dispute. Use of "plaintiff" and "defendant" creates an impersonal tone and provides no specific factual information about the case. Instead, select designations that will be readily understood and also factually informative. Give special attention to distinctive designations in a case involving many parties. In such complex litigation, use of the parties' names will be sufficient only after their relationships have been explained. Use of the parties' formal roles in litigation (for example,

"Appellant" or "Respondent") should be kept to a minimum once the parties have been identified unless a strictly impersonal tone is desired.

Do not hide unfavorable facts, but do not highlight them either. For example, place such facts between prior and subsequent statements of related favorable facts. Conclude with a fact or event favorable to your client's position, not with an unfavorable fact.

Use short sentences to increase readability. Use forceful verbs and nouns, chosen to characterize your client advantageously and to depict events favorably, but not so forceful that a fair-minded reader will lose faith in your credibility. Cases in which one party is always fair and right and the other party is always unfair and wrong are a rarity. Use adjectives sparingly and selectively; avoid adjectives that reflect bias, such as "reactionary" or "hysterical."

Avoid an obtrusive style: let the facts speak for themselves. Do not argue or editorialize. Instead, rely on selection, juxtaposition, and careful word choice for persuasion.

Use diagrams or charts to present complicated facts, relationships, or chronology of events.

After writing the Argument section, review the fact statement. Add any significant facts that were omitted in the first draft. Omit any unnecessary facts that were included. Be certain that you have supported fact statements by accurate references to the record in the form required by governing rules.

§ 9.5 WRITING EFFECTIVE
POINT HEADINGS

A point heading is a concise, persuasive statement of a conclusion or reason that you want the court to accept. Point headings are used as the headings and subheadings within the Argument section of a brief. They are also included in the Table of Contents of the brief to provide a concise summary of the parts of the Argument. Point headings should therefore be written both to persuade and to summarize.

First identify the conclusions that a court must accept in order to decide in your client's favor, then identify reasons that support those conclusions. The general conclusions will be answers to the Questions Presented, but you will also want to identify other specific conclusions that are necessary to acceptance of your client's position.

Next, outline the necessary conclusions. Decide on an order that will, if logically possible, put your strongest points (arguments) at the beginning. Use an order that keeps related parts of the argument together.

Once you have decided on the subject matter and order, write the point headings, using persuasive sentence structure and language. Keep in mind the following generally accepted guidelines for effective point headings.

Use full sentences, not topical phrases.

Unacceptable topical heading:

The alleged contractual relationship.

Use statements about your case, not abstract legal principles.

Unacceptable abstract heading:

A third party is liable for interference with contractual relations only if there is an interference with a valid contractual relationship or business expectancy.

Use statements that demonstrate legal relevance.

Legal relevance not demonstrated:

Plaintiff's evidence failed to establish a valid contractual relationship or business expectancy.

Finally, avoid long, complex statements.

Here is a point heading that demonstrates effective use of these guidelines:

Plaintiff has not proved that Defendant tortiously interfered with his exchange contract because Plaintiff's evidence failed to establish the existence of a valid contractual relationship of the type entitled to protection against interference by third parties.

Notice that this point heading incorporates both the conclusion and the supporting reason. Appoint heading may also state only a conclusion or a reason. Subpoint headings may then supply the supporting reason for a conclusion or the conclusions to be drawn from a reason.

With the above guidelines in mind, compare the following three sets of point headings taken from briefs filed before the United State Supreme Court in *United Steelworks of America v. Weber*, 443 U.S. 193 (1979). Note departures from the guidelines suggested above. Do such lapses influence your understanding of the nature of the case?

1. From Brief for Petitioner–Union:

   I. THE KAISER–USWA SELECTION PRO-
       GRAM DOES NOT VIOLATE TITLE VII.

   A. The Statutory Language

   B. The 1964 Legislative History

      1. The Genesis of the House Bill

      2. The Judiciary Committee Report

      3. The House floor Debate

      4. The Senate

      5. House consideration of the Senate Amend-
   ments

      6. The Interplay Between Title IV and Title VII

         a. The Decision under Title IV

         b. The Link to Title VII

   C. The Meaning of the 1964 Legislative History

   D. The 1972 Legislative History

   II. ALTERNATIVE THEORIES PREMISED
        UPON ASSUMED GOVERNMENTAL POW-
        ERS ARE NOT APPROPRIATE BASES FOR
        DECIDING THIS CASE.

   III. FINAL CONSIDERATIONS

*2. From Brief for the United States and the Equal
     Employment Opportunity Commission:*

The Gramercy training programs are a permissible form of voluntary affirmative action under Title
VII.

   A. Title VII permits, and often requires, employers to
       take race-conscious action.

   B. Devising remedies for discrimination may require consideration of race.

      1. The legislative history of the 1964 Act

      2. The legislative history of the 1972 amendments to Title VII

   C. Title VII permits private parties to take affirmative action to remedy apparent employment discrimination similar to the relief that a court could order to remedy proven discrimination.

   D. Kaiser could reasonably believe it would be found liable for discriminating against blacks at the Gramercy plant.

   E. The Gramercy training programs were appropriate remedies for the apparent Title VII violations in hiring for the craft positions.

   F. Title VII authorizes employers to take affirmative action in response to Executive Order 11246.

      1. The Executive Order program requires government contractors to take affirmative action, without need for proof of prior discrimination by each contractor.

      2. The Executive Order program is consistent with Title VII.

      3. The Gramercy training programs were consistent with the Executive Order program.

3. From an amicus brief:

   I. Title VII Does Not Prohibit an Employer and a Union from Adopting Reasonable Race Conscious Measures to Overcome the Absence of Minorities from Skilled Jobs.

II. The Kaiser–Steelworker Training Agreement is Lawful Under Title VII.

   A. The Record Establishes a Basis for Remedial Action.

   B. The Training Program was a Reasonable response to the Absence of Blacks in Craft Jobs.

§ 9.6 WRITING AN EFFECTIVE SUMMARY OF THE ARGUMENT

Although the summary of the argument is placed before the argument in a brief, it should be written after the argument has been both written and revised. It answers the questions presented as succinctly as possible while outlining the reasoning that supports the answers.

The Supreme Court rules recommend that the summary should be a succinct, accurate, and clear condensation of the argument actually made in the body of the brief. It should not merely repeat the headings. Thus, the summary should be more than a mere assertion of your client's right to win the case. It should present the crux of the argument. It should weave together the strands of argument from the brief and identify the logical relationships between key points. Normally no authorities are discussed, although citations to one or two crucial cases may be included.

The paragraphs of the summary are set off with numerals or letters corresponding to divisions of the argument proper.

§ 9.7 WRITING THE CONCLUSION

A conclusion "specifying with particularity" the relief requested is required by the United States Supreme Court rules. Some counsel believe that the basic arguments should also be briefly summarized again. If such a summary is included, it should be extremely brief. The requested relief should be specified first for the benefit of any judge who might regard a summary as unnecessary repetition. The basic arguments may then be succinctly presented as reasons for granting the requested relief. The relationship between multiple arguments should be identified, as in the following brief conclusion.

The judgment for plaintiff should be reversed. Plaintiff did not have a valid contract or a business expectancy of the type protected against tortuous interference. In the alternative, the conduct of defendant, as a competitor, was privileged.

§ 9.8 THE ARGUMENT: WRITING TO PERSUADE

(a) General Writing Goals

Test your readiness to draft any argument by trying to state in one sentence the conclusion that you want the court to reach. Then attempt to change places with the judges. Ask yourself what you would want to know first if you sat in a judge's chair. How would you want the law presented? As you draft, keep in mind a judge who may be tired, who may be reading your brief after reading others on different subjects, or who may be able to devote only limited time to considering it. Structure your brief from its beginning to its conclusion so that the judge will be able to scan it rapidly and understand your case and your argument quickly. Judges are not always able to study each brief in detail.

Following are other general writing goals to keep in mind while drafting an argument.

Get to the point. Explain what your client wants and why. Tell the court what you want in the first page or two of the brief, not in the middle or at the end. Explain exactly what you want the court to do.

Give the best argument first. Tell the court first the best reason for deciding in your favor. One point—simply, directly, and persuasively argued—is sometimes all you need.

Keep your argument simple. Your case should make sense to the court in terms of everyday life. It should show the court how the people involved may be handled fairly and humanely within the structure of the law.

Be concise. Judges universally complain that briefs are too long. They complain that there is too much laborious, unapplied case analysis and too little effort to revise and condense. From the judge's point of view, shorter is better.

Remember that string citations and multiple cases are rarely helpful and that long quotations from cases and other authorities may not be read.

(b) Controlling Tone

Tone is often overlooked by legal writers. It is never overlooked by readers. Any conspicuous tone interferes with reception of content by causing the reader to react first to the tone and only secondly to the subject matter. That is true whether the tone is informal, stuffy, pretentious, hyperbolic, bitter, casual, or uncertain.

Tone must be carefully monitored in brief writing. Judges may begin to react favorably or unfavorably to the substance of an argument according to the way its tone affects them. This is often a subconscious reaction, making it difficult for the reader to make allowance for an irritating tone.

The following fact statement from a brief submitted for the Petitioner in a recent case demonstrates uncontrolled tone:

> A couple of weeks thereafter, while in flight from crime, he again tried to do himself in a Reno hotel. Furthermore, before entering his guilty plea, he kept on slashing at himself and eating light bulbs. The ingestion of light bulbs also causes doubt as to Petitioner's ability to aid his Counsel.

The tone varies from stuffy ("thereafter," "flight from crime," "ingestion causes doubt") to colloquial ("a couple of," "do himself in," "kept on"), making the fact statement ludicrous. Because the tone is out of control, the court may have difficulty according credibility to the lawyer who submitted it.

The following guidelines can help you control the tone of your briefs.

Establish an assertive or emphatic tone by making direct, not indirect, assertions. Examples of indirect assertions are:: "It appears to be the case that," "It can be argued," "It was clear to the court that," "It is conceivable that," and "One feature of which one should be aware." Do not, however, be aggressive. Do not tell the court what it must do or think. The court will decide for itself what is or is not persuasive authority.

Beware of humor unless you know your audience well. Attempted humor may annoy one or more judges of a court. However, judges, like all readers, appreciate the lightening, sometimes enlightening, effect of figures of speech, examples, and famous sayings–used sparingly. The following example of humor works because it grows directly out of the subject matter (legality of a search of defendant's person):

> When Officer McDonald patted down the Defendant, he discovered nothing but two lobster tails. Officer McDonald testified that he immediately recognized them as lobster tails and immediately knew that they were not weapons. Yet the search did not end with this discovery.... Lobster tails are not contraband; there is no law against carrying concealed lobster tails with or without a sales receipt. Lobster tails are not inherently suspect. Nor do they become suspect because they are frozen or because they bear the label of the store that packaged them.

Do not make the case sound ridiculously easy or opposing counsel sound ridiculously blind. An arrogant or superior tone will not advance your case. For example, a sentence such as, "Cases cited by

Plaintiff are inapposite and easily distinguishable," may offend or annoy the judicial reader who may find the plaintiff's cases difficult to distinguish. Similarly, a court may form a negative opinion of a writer who facetiously uses the pronoun "one" to attack opposing counsel. "One is really at a loss to see how this argument can even be made" or "A reading of Plaintiff's Memorandum to the Court leaves one with a certain sense of confusion." Sarcasm is never appropriate. Neither is an insulting or intemperate tone, however much opposing counsel deserves it.

Avoid informality, especially as expressed in colloquialism, for example, "Whoever would have thought that Mr. Jarvis would go and shoot him!" Colloquial terms or phrases are imprecise by nature; they have no fixed meanings. Informal abbreviations like "ad," "auto," "cite," "exam," "gas," "memo," "phone," and "quote" are also inappropriate. On the other hand, avoid excessive formality. Stuffiness, as much as chumminess, distracts the reader from your ideas.

Use "we" for yourself and your client, and use "counsel for appellant or respondent" for opposing counsel. Do not use "you" to refer to the court. Do not use "I" to refer to yourself.

(c) Using Rhetorical Devices for Persuasion

Rhetorical devices are means of achieving emphasis through special sentence structure, paragraph design, and wording. Many of these devices are explained elsewhere in this *Nutshell*. The most effective devices are illustrated in this subsection.

The key to effective use of any rhetorical device is subtlety: the device must appear natural. It must not attract attention as a gimmick being used on the reader. The exception is the appeal to logic. That rhetorical appeal is more effective if it is obvious. Appeals to emotion, in contrast, will fail if obvious.

(1) Achieving Emphasis With Sentence Structures

A.   Place important words at the beginning and at the end of sentences. Use short sentences for special emphasis as in the following example.

> Whether surveillance is electronic, optical, or human is irrelevant where there is no reasonable expectation of privacy. While on a public street, the defendant had no such reasonable expectation.

In a conspicuous position, understatement is more effective than overstatement. The above example would be less effective if the words "clearly," "certainly," or "obviously" were added ("the defendant obviously had no such reasonable expectation").

B.   Avoid beginning a sentence with an equivocation, such as, "it would seem to be" or "it may be that." Instead, write forcefully "it must follow that," or simply begin with the point itself and then state necessary qualifications.

C. Put subordinate thoughts in less emphatic positions. Compare this pair of sentences:

The result is that enforcement of the rescission right is not uniform among the circuit courts. (The phrase "among circuit courts" receives undue emphasis.)

The result is that enforcement of the rescission right among the circuit courts is not uniform. (The important words "result" and "is not uniform" receive the emphasis they deserve.)

D. Use active voice for forcefulness, as discussed in Chapter 4.

E. Make affirmative assertions. Even negative ideas can be expressed in positive, therefore more forceful, form.

The approach of the English courts is somewhat uncertain and less clear-cut than that of the American courts.

Revised: The approach of the American courts is more clearly defined than that of the English courts.

F. Use double negatives sparingly for understatement. The double negative, such as "not infrequently," has a respectable history as a rhetorical device for emphasis. Although it has fallen out of favor, it may still be employed on occasion as a means of understatement. For example, "not wholly unsuccessful" understates a lack of success, thus emphasizing it, as compared to its affirmative form "partially successful," which emphasizes a degree of success.

G. Use parallel constructions to draw attention to similar ideas.

In *Cooper* the court considered damage to a number of motor cars caused by the negligence of a painting contractor. In *Runnels* the court considered damage to construction machinery caused by the negligence of the mechanic who repaired it.

H. Use parallel constructions for rhetorical effect. Similarity of structure in a pair or series of related words, phrases, or clauses will make them more memorable. ("He tried to make the law clear, precise, and equitable.") The principle of parallelism is that like things be phrased in like terms.

Variations of parallelism include:

1. Repetition of the same word or group of words at the beginning of successive clauses (anaphora): "They were common, though prohibited by law. They were common, though condemned by public opinion." This scheme establishes rhythm and produces a strong emotional effect.

2. Repetition of the same word or group of words at the ends of successive clauses (epistrophe): "To the good American many subjects are sacred: children are sacred, business is sacred, property is sacred." This scheme sets up a pronounced rhythm with special emphasis resulting from repetition of words and placement of words in the emphatic final position.

3. Repetition of last word of one clause at the beginning of the following clause (anadiplosis): "The crime was common; common be the pain."

4. Repetition of words, in successive clauses, in reverse grammatical order (antimetabole): "One should work to live, not live to work." Antimetabole gives the air of the neatly turned phrase.

5. Juxtaposition of contrasting ideas, often in parallel structure (antithesis): "Though argumentative, he was modest." The opposition in an antithesis can reside either in words or in ideas, or both.

I. Rhetorical questions, that is, questions to which no immediate reply is expected, may be used sparingly as emphatic variations of affirmative statements.

Did Mr. Bertleson have a right to use his easement in accordance with the express language of his covenant?

(2) Achieving Emphasis With Paragraphing

A. Use persuasive paragraph structure. In each section of a brief or in each paragraph, state your argument or position first—not your opponent's— and state it affirmatively. Then dispense with your opponent's argument. To make paragraphs affirmative: (i) State your argument or position first. (ii) Acknowledge contrary evidence, or state the opposing argument in the middle of the paragraph. (iii) Refute contrary evidence or opposing argument. (iv) Restate your argument as a conclusion.

One purpose of this structure is to put favorable arguments and facts in the most conspicuous place (the beginning and the end). The interior of a paragraph should contain less important elements. Both unfavorable facts and arguments must be included, of course, but they will be given less emphasis in the middle of a paragraph.

Another purpose of this structure is to give a balanced analysis of the issue, that is, to reflect fair consideration of both sides even if only one is fully developed in the paragraph.

Example of an unpersuasive paragraph structure:

Warwick v. Woodinville Company, 100 Wash. 200, 174 P. 15 (1920), however, represents an archaic view of "publication," and it may not be binding precedent today. More recent cases adopt the rule that to establish defamation when information is circulated among those with a "common interest" requires a showing of malice or bad faith. Applied here, if false medical information were circulated among supervisors evaluating an employee, a common interest in the information would probably be established. The complaining party would be required to show that the false statement was made with malice or in bad faith. See, e.g., *Sam v. Painter's Local Union*, 40 Wn.2d 800, 200 P.2d 754 (1955). Even though false medical information was circulated among Company personnel, who see the material in the course of their normal duties, the lack of evidence of bad faith distinguishes this case from *Warwick*.

In the above example, both unfavorable authority and an unfavorable fact appear in positions of emphasis. Recent authority and the present requirements for establishing defamation should be emphasized instead, as in the following revision.

Revised: Plaintiff has presented no evidence of malice or bad faith and therefore has not established that defamatory statements were made. A showing of malice or bad faith is necessary to establish defamation when allegedly false information is circulated among persons with a "common interest." See *e.g., Sam v. Painter's Local Union*, 40 Wn.2d 800, 200 P.2d 754 (1955). Such "common interest" can be found in Defendant's circulation of medical information among supervisors evaluating an employee because the supervisors see the information in the course of their normal duties. Plaintiff's primary case, *Warwick v. Woodinville Company*, 100 Wash. 200, 174 P. 15 (192), was decided before the court required evidence of malice or bad faith under these circumstances. Having failed to present evidence of malice or bad faith, Plaintiff has not satisfied present requirements for establishing defamation.

B. Use short paragraphs for emphasis. A short paragraph, like a short, climactic sentence, provides emphasis automatically. A one-sentence paragraph will provide extra emphasis, but only if used sparingly and skillfully. The following example illustrates effective use of a one-sentence paragraph.

Plaintiff's brief does not refer to the Plan itself. Rather, Plaintiff ignores the legal text and argues on the basis of a summary description of the Plan contained in a booklet, "Company Employee Retirement Plan." The booklet states that it is a summary and that "for a proper understanding of the Plan, the complete text should be read."

Construction of the Plan is controlled by its legal text, not by selective citations from a summary booklet.

(3) *Achieving Emphasis With Language*

"Now, words in their proper order are the raw material of the law, and words have a magic of their own; they have color and sound and meaning and associations. But choice words in the right order have a more magical power still.''—Birkett, *Law and Literature: The Equipment of the Lawyer*, 36 A.B.A.J. 891, 946 (1950) (Excerpted with permission from the American Bar Association Journal.)

A. Remember to consider word connotation. Words create impressions. The writer's task is to choose words that create the appropriate impressions for his or her persuasive purpose. While writing each word, keep your objective in mind: For example, are you trying to establish guilt, liability, a violation of constitutional rights?

Nouns: Nouns have negative or positive connotations; use them carefully and purposefully.

Positive	*Negative*
offense	crime
offender	criminal
control	coercion
debate	argument
reconstruction	fabrication
eminence	notoriety
adversary	enemy
rapid disassembly	explosion

Verbs: Verbs provide the most subtle, thus the most effective, coloration. Statements may be "affirmed" (implies trust), "asserted" (neutral), or "alleged" (implies doubt). The verb "sever," for example, makes a stronger impression than the verbs "cut" and "break."

Use active verbs, such as "conceal," "ignore," and "intend" rather than forms of the weak verb "to be" or its substitutes, "seem," "become," "exist," "appear," "arise," "relate to," "deal with," "involve," and "concern."

Adjectives: Use a minimum of these because they are less subtle than either nouns or verbs. Do not pile up similar adjectives like "inequitable and unconscionable." If an adjective is necessary, use only one and choose it carefully. As Voltaire remarked, the adjective is the enemy of the noun.

B. Use ornamental language cautiously. While neither lawyers nor their clients are willing to pay for literary skill for its own sake, one mark of an expert legal writer is the ability to use vivid examples, interesting similes, metaphors, or analogies. This ability grows out of a sensitivity to language, to how it sounds, and to what auditory and visual effects it has on the reader. It grows out of an awareness of human nature. Prose that delights us also instructs us more efficiently and effectively than writing that deadens our senses.

The ability to use figurative language skillfully develops over a lifetime of writing. The ability may, however, be cultivated by paying attention to the sensory dimension of words. Metaphors and similes should be fresh. Do not mix metaphors, for example, "We need this case like a horse needs a fifth wheel"; "when we come to that bridge, we will swim over it"; "they smelled a rat and nipped it in the bud"; or "they built their argument on fuzzy ground." Clichés should be avoided unless "renovated" (for example, "no truer words were ever silenced").

C. Avoid unpersuasive words and ineffective rhetorical devices that may weaken the power of your arguments. Avoid using "clear" and "clearly" in a brief. These do not persuade the court that the case is clearly in your favor or even clear at all. These overused words may irritate the judicial reader. "Obvious" and "obviously" are similarly objectionable.

Avoid expressions of supposed candor, modesty, or any other attempts at personal expression. Some of the worst examples are: "frankly," "to be frank," "to be honest," "with all candor," "candidly," "I humbly disagree," "I do not pretend to be an expert."

Do not use words sarcastically or ironically to mean something other than their dictionary meaning. For example, in this sentence taken from a state supreme court brief, the word "remarkable" might boomerang on its author if the court agrees with the contention:

> Plaintiffs make the remarkable contention that the "well-established doctrine of restraint" is the appropriate rule.

Avoid words made trite by overuse. Both psychological terms and computer jargon have become trite and have a negative effect on many readers. The following words, among many others, have been degraded by imprecise use and overuse: actualize, appropriate, definitive, effectuate, duplicative, finalize, impact (as a noun or as a verb), implement (as verb), interactive, interface, input, meaningful dialogue, ongoing, optimize, qualitative, quantitative, quality (as adjective), relevant, replicate, synchronization, update (as noun or verb), viable.

(4) Using Classical Devices for Persuasion

The devices for persuasion have not changed since they were studied and described by the Greeks. Three of the more important of these devices are discussed below.

A. Logical Appeal. Although the emotional and ethical appeal should never be ignored, the logical appeal is the most important and persuasive for the advocate. The logical appeal in legal writing is chiefly an appeal to precedent. Like cases are logically decided alike. The writer's task is to demonstrate the similarity or dissimilarity of decided cases with the client's case.

B. Emotional and Ethical Appeals. Remember that argumentative writing affects a reader's emotions and conveys an image of the author. Too often law students and lawyers aim only at a reader's logical mind and forget to consider the reader's emotions. After you have identified the result you want, identify the emotion or combination of emotions that will lead the reader to that result. Select the details of your case that will arouse that emotion: these should be subtly emphasized in your argument.

Any writer is more persuasive if the reader respects her or him. This respect, traditionally called the ethical appeal, emerges from what is written as well as from how it is written. An image of honesty and straightforwardness should emerge, beginning with the fact statement. The writer should set forth the facts and all that follows in a well balanced and reasonable way. The writer must not appear to be blinded by emotion. Nor should the writer be timid or apologetic. The best image for a brief writer is that of a strong but reasonable counselor, unafraid of taking a stand but not willing to exaggerate or contort the facts or law to make a point.

Brief-writers inevitably find weak spots in their own cases. A good rule of thumb is to be critical of your case before the reader is. Acknowledge and then overcome obvious weaknesses through authority, policy, or reason. Account for weaknesses in your case before your reader discovers them. You will thus create an image of objectivity, while simultaneously making an appeal to the reason and logic of your reader.

Sophisticated brief-writers sometimes make educated allusions to historical events or people or repeat famous aphorisms and thus convey an image of urbanity and broadmindedness. A novice should avoid such risky flourishes. It is enough to establish an image of reasonableness by reflecting your understanding of both sides of a case, by conceding small points when necessary, and by acknowledging the possible validity of the opposing argument while undercutting it.

(5) *Avoiding Ineffective Emphasis*

Mechanical contrivances like italics, underlining, boldface type, dashes, and exclamation marks should not normally be used for emphasis. (For appropriate use of italics, dashes and exclamation marks, see Chapter 6). In typewritten text, underlining does provide a clear visual signal to the reader. Thus, underlining may be useful in certain writing situations, always provided that it is used carefully and sparingly.

§ 9.9 THE FINAL TOUCH

Careful revision from a printed draft is essential. Print out your draft, then follow the suggestions in Chapter 4 for shortening sentences and eliminating unnecessary words. Brief writing is often a misnomer: briefs are rarely "brief." As all writers know, brevity takes more time than verbosity. Your brief writing will be more persuasive if it is lean and sharply focused.

＊

SELECTED REFERENCES

GENERAL COMPOSITION AND GRAMMAR

J. Opdycke, *Harper's English Grammar* (1983).

The most comprehensive and reliable guide to grammar available to the non-specialist. Available in paperback.

Strunk and White, *The Elements of Style* (4th ed. 1999).

A concise and widely used paperback guide to general writing. Useful as an introduction to popular discourse; parts of the style section not helpful for legal writing.

LANGUAGE

W. Burton, *Legal Thesaurus* (3rd ed. 1998).

A useful source of inspiration for synonyms and associated legal concepts for more than 5,000 words in legal contexts.

W. Follett, *Modern American Usage: A Guide* (Hill & Wang, l998).

Fowler's Modern English Usage (2d ed., Oxford Univ. Press, 2003).

D. Mellinkoff, *The Language of the Law* (1963).

A fine historical approach to legal language, written by a lawyer. Entertaining and instructive.

LEGAL RESEARCH AND ANALYSIS

M. Rombauer, *Legal Problem Solving: Analysis, Research and Writing* (5th ed. 1992).

CITATIONS AND MECHANICS

A Uniform System of Citation (17th ed. 2000).

Published and distributed by the Harvard Law Review Association, this "Blue Book" is the final guide on structure, content, and form of legal citations and on some rules of mechanics (abbreviations, numerals, symbols, italicization, capitalization, and court titles).

RHETORIC

E. Corbett, *Classical Rhetoric for the Modern Student* (4th ed. Oxford Univ. Press, 1998).

A compilation of the classical techniques for persuasion and argument. Much of it is directly applicable to argumentative legal writing. Contains a section on judicial discourse.

INDEX

_____

**Italics indicate references to explanations
of word usages**

References are to Pages.

_____

227

†